· The Field Guide to ·

Farmall Tractors

Text by Robert N. Pripps
Photographs by Andrew Morland

Voyageur Press

Dedication

To Jean Poyser, the late wife of Norval Poyser, both passionate collectors of Farmall tractors and International Harvester memorabilia.

Edited by Kari Cornell
Designed by Andrea Rud
Printed in China

04   05   06   07   08   5   4   3   2   1

Library of Congress Cataloging-in-Publication Data
Pripps, Robert N., 1932-
  The field guide to Farmall tractors / text by Robert N. Pripps ;
photographs by Andrew Morland.
      p. cm.
Includes index.
  ISBN 0-89658-558-1 (hardcover)
  1. IHC tractors—History. I. Title.
  TL233.6.I38P7523 2004
  629.225—dc22

                            2003019476

Distributed in Canada by Raincoast Books, 9050 Shaughnessy Street, Vancouver, B.C. V6P 6E5

Published by Voyageur Press, Inc.
123 North Second Street, P.O. Box 338, Stillwater, MN 55082 U.S.A.
651-430-2210, fax 651-430-2211
books@voyageurpress.com
www.voyageurpress.com

Educators, fundraisers, premium and gift buyers, publicists, and marketing managers: Looking for creative products and new sales ideas? Voyageur Press books are available at special discounts when purchased in quantities, and special editions can be created to your specifications. For details contact the marketing department at 800-888-9653.

On the title page: *This 1955 Farmall 400 is the rare high-clearance version equipped with the Torque Amplifier dual-range power-shift gearbox. Owner: Walter Keller, Brillion, Wisconsin*

Contents

Introduction

Author Robert N. Pripps on a 1938 F-20

Farmall—the name itself conjures an image of the quintessential farm tractor, although for each of us that image might be different. I suppose most, like myself, would see the bright red Farmall H or M. Others might think of the gray, utilitarian F-20 on steel. Younger Farmall enthusiasts might see big tractors with cabs and dual-drive wheels. Whatever comes to mind, the Farmall name is an essential part of farm heritage, and the giant Farmall 1468 of 1973 is related to the earliest Farmall Regular of 1924. This book covers the more than fifty different Farmall models built during the tractor's more than fifty-year run. A word of thanks goes to the collectors of the beautifully restored Farmalls shown on the following pages. Not only did these collectors go through a lot of trouble getting the tractors out for us, even washing some and moving them around for the best light, but they often introduced us to friends who also owned Farmalls and invited us to photograph them. These are the true Farmall experts. Without the knowledge they shared, this book would be mighty thin.

Also, thanks to authors who paved the way with the excellent International Harvester books that I used as references: Randy Leffingwell, Cyrus McCormick, Ralph Sanders, Ken Updike, and Chuck Wendel; and a special thanks to the State Historical Society of Wisconsin and Margaret Hafstad.

A photographer like Andrew Morland makes his job look easy, but capturing quality images is no simple task. It requires technical aptitudes for lenses, shutters, film types and lighting, as well as artistic sensitivity. Andrew took approximately fifty exposures for every one appearing in this book, using up to three different Nikon camera bodies and a bag full of lenses, and a heavy-duty tripod for every shot. I think you will agree his efforts paid off, even if in some cases the weather did not cooperate.

Finally, a special thanks to Voyageur Press and Editorial Director Michael Dregni. Michael has guided almost all of my twenty-some books through the production process, making them read and look as good as they do. If you are not already on the mailing list for Voyageur's catalogs, my advice would be to get on the list as quickly as you can so you don't miss any of their great offerings.

Robert N. Pripps
Springstead, Wisconsin
2003

The Farmall F-20 made harvest time much more manageable.

The 1972 Farmall 1468 used a V-8 diesel of 550-ci (9,013-cc) displacement supplied by the truck division of International Harvester. The twin straight pipes provide a special touch of class. Owner: Wilson Gatewood

1938 Farmall F-20

The 1939 Model M was the top of the line of Loewy-styled Farmalls. With its powerful four-cylinder engine, it was rated for three plows.

The popular Farmall 340 was built from 1958 through 1963.

Chapter 1

The Original Farmall and Its Derivatives

The Farmall Regular, F-20, H, Super H, 300, 350, 340, 404

The Farmall Regular, 1924–1932

At first, when there was only one Farmall, it was simply called the "Farmall." It was not called the "Regular" until the Fairway version came out in 1926. The "Regular" moniker was then unofficially adopted to help differentiate between the two.

The original Farmall was quite a long time a-bornin', beginning life as various motor cultivator prototypes built between 1915 and 1920. At first, the idea of an all-purpose tractor designed to replace both the horse and the steam engine met with considerable internal resistance at Harvester. Sales management personnel thought it would take away from the sales of the profitable conventional tractors. But in the early 1920s, when the Fordson tractor knocked International Harvester out of first place in tractor sales, Harvester management quickly brought out the Farmall as an all-purpose farm tractor. It plowed, cultivated, and powered implements through the flat belt or the rear-mounted PTO. The capable Farmall soon restored IH to first place in tractor sales.

The first all-purpose versions of 1921 were reversible. The drive wheels went first for haymaking, corn picking and the like, while the small "steering" wheels went first for cultivating crops. By 1922, Harvester abandoned the reversible idea, and the Farmall began to look like a "Farmall." Although the people developing the tractor called it by the name "Farmall" as early as 1919, the name wasn't registered as a trademark until 1923. Even then, skeptics of the concept prevented the use of the name externally until 1924, when the first Farmalls were sold to the public.

Early Farmalls had automatic steering brakes. The tractor was equipped with individual hand brakes, but to allow the operator to both steer and raise the cultivator at the end of a row, cables actuated by the steering apparatus applied the brake on the side toward which the turn was being made.

Right and following pages: *The Regular was little changed from its introduction in 1924 until the end of its run in 1932. This is a 1930 model. Owner: Larry Kinsey of Indiana*

Models and Variations		Serial Numbers: Regular	
Model	Years Built	Beginning S/N	Year
Regular	1924–1932	QC501	1924
		QC701	1925
Specifications: Regular		QC1539	1926
Engine: Four-cylinder		T1569	1927
Fuel: Kerosene		T15471	1928
Bore & stroke: 3.75x5.00 inches		T40370	1929
(95.25x127 mm)		T75691	1930
Displacement: 220.9 ci (3,620 cc)		T117784	1931
Engine speed: 1,200 rpm		T131872	1932
Power: 20.05 PTO hp			
Transmission: Three speeds forward			
Weight: 4,100 pounds (1,860 kg)			

The 1924 Farmall was the first tractor to feature the tricycle configuration, with its close-set front wheels and large-diameter rears. Owner: Harry Lee, Elnora, Indiana

The Farmall F-20, 1932–1939

After eight years of production with only minor year-by-year changes, Harvester brought out the much-improved F-20 version. Engine improvements gave it three more horsepower, and a four-speed transmission replaced the three-speed unit of the Regular. It was available with wide or narrow rear-wheel treads. Buyers also had the option of a wide front or a single front wheel instead of the standard dual tricycle front. F-20 production ended in 1939, although some were assembled from parts and sold in 1940.

Farmalls were painted gray until late 1936, when bright Farmall Red tractors took their place. Rubber tires became an option in 1935. The cable-actuated steering brakes were replaced on the 1939 models with left and right foot brakes close together on the right side of the platform.

The 1936 F-20 featured about 15 percent more power than the Regular, although the engine displacement remained the same at 221 ci (3,622 cc). Owner: Ron Hattendorf, Genoa, Illinois

Models and Variations

Model	Years Built
F-20	1932–1939

Specifications: Model F-20

Engine: Four-cylinder
Fuel: Kerosene
Bore & stroke: 3.75x5.00 inches
  (95.25x127 mm)
Displacement: 220.9 ci (3,620 cc)
Engine speed: 1,200 rpm
Power: 23.11 PTO hp
Transmission: Four speeds forward
Weight: 4,545 pounds (2,062 kg)

Specifications: Model F-20

Engine: Four-cylinder
Fuel: Distillate
Bore & stroke: 3.75x5.00 inches
  (95.25x127 mm)
Displacement: 220.9 ci (3,620 cc)
Engine speed: 1,200 rpm
Power: 26.78 PTO hp
Transmission: Four speeds forward
Weight: 4,400 pounds (1,996 kg)

Serial Numbers: Model F-20

Beginning S/N	Year
FA/TA501	1932
FA/TA3001	1933
TA135000 (to 135661)	1934
TA6832	1935
TA32716	1936
TA68749	1937
TA105597	1938
TA130865 (to 134999)	1939
TA135700	1939

During 1932, the F-20 replaced the Regular. This 1934 model has a four-speed transmission and a 15 percent increase in horsepower. Owner: Steve Wade, Plainwell, Michigan

Changes to the 1939 F-20 included moving the brakes to the right side of the platform where they could be locked together for use as a service brake.

All photos and following page: *This wide-front 1938 F-20 has an aftermarket starter and generator installation. It also has the optional half rear fenders. The wide-front version was only available with the narrow rear tread. Owner: John Wagner*

McCORMICK-DEERING

FARMALL 20—

The Original Successful Row-Crop All-Purpose Tractor

IN the illustration you see the Farmall 20—essentially the original Farmall all-purpose row-crop cultivating tractor but with the latest improvements and a good ten per cent more power.

The Farmall, when released for sale in 1924 after nearly 10 years of painstaking research and experimentation, was the first tractor of any make to successfully adapt the tireless efficiency of mechanical power to every major farm operation, notably the previously unheard of tractor-cultivation of growing corn. This is the tractor that with its specially designed, patented equipment revolutionized crop-growing methods, not only in the great corn and cotton belts but in all other sections where crops are planted, cultivated, and harvested in rows. In the annals of power farming the final perfection of the Farmall tractor principle and initiation of the Farmall system of farming will remain a brilliant historical achievement and a triumph of International Harvester engineering.

Any of the ordinary farm implements can be pulled behind a Farmall but its maximum time- and labor-saving effectiveness is attained only through using the full line of special Farmall equipment designed to work with it. A score of patents on Farmall tractors and their attachments explain why Farmall performance cannot be duplicated by any other tractor. Outstanding among these exclusive features are the steering-wheel-controlled cultivator gang quick shift, the steering-wheel-controlled automatic square or pivot turn, and the forward location of the cultivator gangs.

These and numerous other exclusive Farmall features are explained in Farmall folders which are yours for the asking. Just mark and mail the post card on page 31.

WHAT THE F-20 WILL DO:

☛ 1. Will perform virtu-ally every power operation on row-crop farms of 125 to 200 acres or more. ☛ 2. Will do the work of 8 to 12 horses or mules for considerably less money. Will work from daylight till dark, if nec-essary, at sustained speeds of approximately 2 to 4 miles per hour. ☛ 3. Will work all day on from 18 to 24 gallons of fuel (regularly equipped to use gasoline or No. 1 distil-late). ☛ 4. Will plow 7 to 12 acres a day; plant (4-row) 40 to 50 acres; cultivate 40 to 60 acres; mow 20 to 30 acres; pick (2-row) 14 to 18 acres; drive a 22-inch thresher; and do other field and belt work in proportion.

Special high-speed transmission available for rubber-tired trac-tors. Recommended tire sizes: front 6.00-16, rear 11.25-28 and 9.00-36.

FULL SPECIFICATIONS ON PAGES 16 AND 17

PAGE 7

This page from a vintage McCormick-Deering tractor catalog touts the many benefits of the F-20.

The Farmall H, 1939–1953

The Farmall H was introduced in 1939 as a replacement for the F-20. The H was one of the first products of industrial designer Raymond Loewy, who was hired to restyle the entire International Harvester line. Loewy was also responsible for the rakish Studebaker car styling of 1953 as well as for the famous Air Force One paint scheme first seen in 1962. Loewy's use of smooth contours and bright red sheet metal make even a 1939 Farmall look completely modern more than sixty years later. Production continued until 1953 with almost 400,000 units sold.

The new Farmall H had a modern, higher-speed engine with water pump cooling and magneto ignition. The H featured a five-speed transmission, and buyers could choose models that ran on either gasoline or distillate fuel. A starter and electrical system were optional. Keyway rear-axle wheel spacing was new on the H, providing spreads of 44–80 inches (111.76–203.2 cm).

The frame layout allowed the mounting of cultivators and other implements that would also fit on the H's big brother, the Farmall M. While the dual tricycle front end was standard, a wide front was optional. High-clearance, or HV, models were also available.

Models and Variations

Model	Years Built
H	1939-1953

Specifications: Model H
Engine: Four-cylinder
Fuel: Gasoline
Bore & stroke: 3.375x4.25 inches
  (85.73x107.95 mm)
Displacement: 152 ci (2,491 cc)
Engine speed: 1,650 rpm
Power: 24.28 PTO hp
Transmission: Five speeds forward
Weight: 5,500 pounds (2,495 kg)

Specifications: Model H
Engine: Four-cylinder
Fuel: Kerosene
Bore & stroke: 3.375x4.25 inches
  (85.73x107.95 mm)
Displacement: 152 ci (2,491 cc)
Engine speed: 1,650 rpm
Power: 22.14 PTO hp
Transmission: Five speeds forward
Weight: 5,550 pounds (2,517 kg)

Serial Numbers: Model H (FBH/FBI IV)

Beginning S/N	Year
501	1939
10653	1940
52387	1941
93237	1942
122590	1943
150251	1944
186123	1945
214820	1946
241143	1947
268991	1948
300876	1949
327975	1950
351923	1951
375961	1952
390500 (391730 last)	1953

Above: *This 1940 Farmall H was built with steel wheels and without a starter, generator, or implement lift. The four-cylinder OHV engine produced about 25 horsepower on gasoline.*

Right: *This ad for the Farmall H appeared in the February 1942 issue of* Farm Journal.

Above and following pages: *The 1946 Farmall H, designed by Raymond Loewy, was aesthetically pleasing and functional. The tractor featured a modern high-speed engine of 152 ci (2,491 cc) operating at 1,650 rpm. Owner and restorer: Jeremy Sevcik of Northfield, Minnesota*

The DF-25, built in Neuss, Germany, from 1951 to 1953, is roughly equivalent to the U.S. Farmall H. This 1952 model has a four-cylinder diesel engine of 125 ci (2,048 cc), rated at 25 hp. Owner: Johann Hood

The Super H, 1953–1954

The Farmall Super H was much the same as the H, except Harvester increased the cylinder bore by 0.125 inch (3.175 mm), giving the "Super" about 25 percent more horsepower. Ball-ramp disk rear brakes were also new on the Super H. Later in the model run, the battery was moved to a location under the seat. Live hydraulics was an option. The distillate fuel option was not available on the Super H. Super H production began in late 1953 and continued until late 1954. A few less than 22,000 were delivered, making the Super H quite collectable.

The 1953 Super H had almost 30 percent more power than the standard H, as the engine displacement had been increased to 164 ci (2,687 cc) from 152 ci (2,491 cc).

Models and Variations

Model	Years Built
Super H	1953–1954

Specifications: Super H

Engine: Four-cylinder
Fuel: Gasoline
Bore & stroke: 3.50x 4.25 inches (88.9x107.95 mm)
Displacement: 164 ci (2,687 cc)
Engine speed: 1,650 rpm
Power: 31.30 PTO hp
Transmission: Five speeds forward
Weight: 6,700 pounds (3,039 kg)

Serial Numbers: Super H

Beginning S/N	Year
501	1953
22202	1954

The 1955 German Farmall DGD4 is comparable to the Super H. The DGD4 used a four-cylinder diesel of 133 ci (2,179 cc) rated at 30 horsepower. Owner: Johann Hood

The Farmall 300, 1955–1957

When the Farmall 300 replaced the Super H in 1955 (production actually began in late 1954), Harvester incorporated real improvements. An increase in the engine bore diameter of 0.0625 inch (1.587 mm), plus increasing the rated speed of 100 rpm, provided about 20 percent more horsepower. The five-speed transmission remained, but the optional Torque Amplifier power-shift auxiliary gave ten speeds forward and two in reverse. The International two-point Fast-Hitch was a new option on this model, making changing from one implement to another faster and easier. The advantages of mounted implements over the drawn type had been well proven by tractors using the Ferguson three-point system. Fast-Hitch–equipped Farmalls generally featured front wheel weights. And, a live PTO (also optional) was certainly a great improvement.

Options for the Model 300 included a wide front end, high-clearance versions, and a LPG (liquefied petroleum gas) fuel system with a higher-compression head.

The 300 replaced the Super H in 1955. This 1956 model had a new 169-ci (2,769-cc) engine with an increase of 5 ci (82 cc) over the Super H. Owner: Austin Hurst, Lafayette, California

Models and Variations

Model	Years Built
300	1955–1956

Specifications: Model 300

Engine: Four-cylinder
Fuel: Gasoline
Bore & stroke: 3.563x4.25 inches
   (90.5x107.95 mm)
Displacement: 169 ci (2,769 cc)
Engine speed: 2,000 rpm
Power: 35.99 PTO hp
Transmission: Ten speeds forward
   (with T/A)
Weight: 8,337 pounds (3,782 kg)

Serial Numbers: Model 300

Beginning S/N	Year
501	1954
3360	1955
23224	1956

The Farmall 350, 1957–1958

Again, after only a two-year production run, the 350 replaced the 300 in late 1956. The 350 was essentially the same as the 300, except for a light cream-colored grille and a white Farmall decal on the hood side panels. The Fast-Hitch system featured an improvement called the "Pilot Guide," an implement depth indicator that told the driver how close the plow (or other implement) was running to the desired depth. The Pilot Guide was mounted to the left side of the instrument panel so the driver did not have to look back to check the plow.

The 350 was available in gasoline, LPG, and diesel versions. International Harvester increased the displacement of the gasoline and LPG engines to 175 ci (2,868 cc) by enlarging the bore 0.125 inch (3.175 mm). Harvester also offered the 350 with a new diesel by Continental Motors which displaced 193 ci (3,163 cc). IH had a new diesel in development, but it was not quite ready. The dependable Continental unit filled the bill for the two years the 350 was on the market.

Models and Variations

Model	Years Built
350 G	1957–1958
350 L	1957–1958
350 D	1957–1958

Specifications: Model 350 G
Engine: Four-cylinder
Fuel: Gasoline
Bore & stroke: 3.625x4.25 inches
  (92.1x107.95 mm)
Displacement: 175 ci (2,868 cc)
Engine speed: 1,750 rpm
Power: 39.31 PTO hp
Transmission: Ten speeds forward
  (with T/A)
Weight: 8,339 pounds (3,783 kg)

Specifications: Model 350 L
Engine: Four-cylinder
Fuel: LPG
Bore & stroke: 3.625x4.25 inches
  (92.1x107.95 mm)
Displacement: 175 ci (2,868 cc)
Engine speed: 1,750 rpm
Power: 39.34 PTO hp
Transmission: Ten speeds forward
  (with T/A)
Weight: 8,171 pounds (3,706 kg)

Specifications: Model 350 D
Engine: Four-cylinder
Fuel: Diesel
Bore & stroke: 3.75x4.375 inches
  (95.25x111.125 mm)
Displacement: 193 ci (3,163 cc)
Engine speed: 1,750 rpm
Power: 38.65 PTO hp
Transmission: Ten speeds forward
  (with T/A)
Weight: 8,289 pounds (3,760 kg)

Serial Numbers: Model 350

Beginning S/N	Year
501	1956
1004	1957
14175	1958

Above and following pages: *The Farmall 350 replaced the 300 in 1956, and this is a 1957 model. Displacement on the gasoline and LPG 350s was now up to 175 ci (2,868 cc) from 169 ci (2,769 cc).*

The Farmall 340, 1958–1963

The Farmall 340 was built from late 1958 through 1963. Although it looked somewhat like a modernized 240, the Farmall 340 was all new. A new hydraulic system used transmission oil like the Fords and Fergusons. And, similar to those makes, the pump was located in the transmission case, but a pump on the engine was an option. Another option was the Ferguson-type three-point hitch, rather than the Farmall Fast-Hitch. The Tel-A-Depth implement depth indicator and the IH Traction-Control (similar to the Ferguson Draft Control) were also options. Power steering, while available on the International version of the 340, was not available on the Farmall version. The 340 featured a 12-volt electrical system.

A new 135-ci (2,212-cc) gasoline four-cylinder engine powered the 340, with a 166-ci (2,720-cc) four-cylinder diesel as an option. The 340 had a five-speed transmission, and the Torque Amplifier power shift was available.

The 340, unveiled in 1958, had a totally new design and was available in gasoline or diesel versions. The gasoline type shown here has the C-135 (135 ci/2,212 cc) four-cylinder with overhead valves. Owner: Hal Beitlich, Rockford, Illinois

Models and Variations

Model	Years Built
340 G	1958–1963
340 D	1958–1963

Specifications: Model 340 G

Engine: Four-cylinder
Fuel: Gasoline
Bore & stroke: 3.25x4.125 inches
(82.55x3175 mm)
Displacement: 134.8 ci (2,209 cc)
Engine speed: 2,000 rpm
Power: 32.3 PTO hp
Transmission: Ten speeds forward
(with T/A)
Weight: 6,761 pounds (3,067 kg)

Specifications: Model 340 D

Engine: Four-cylinder
Fuel: Diesel
Bore & stroke: 3.6875x3.875 inches
(93.66x98.43 mm)
Displacement: 165.5 ci (2,712 cc)
Engine speed: 2,000 rpm
Power: 38.93 PTO hp
Transmission: Ten speeds forward
(with T/A)
Weight: 7,579 pounds (3,438 kg)

Serial Numbers: Model 340

Beginning S/N	Year
501	1958
2723	1959
5411	1960
6642	1961
7626	1962
7699	1963

The 1961 340's new diesel engine displaced 166 ci (2,720 cc), rather than the 135 ci (2,212 cc) of the gasoline version. Both were four-cylinder engines of the OHV type. Owner: Wilson Gatewood, Noblesville, Indiana

The Farmall 404, 1961–1967

IH introduced the Farmall 404 as a 1961 model. Production continued through 1967 (the International version continued for another year). The 404 featured the C-135 four-cylinder engine with 134.8 ci (2,209 cc), and a four-speed transmission with a two-range auxiliary instead of the Torque Amplifier power shift. An LPG option was available, but Harvester did not offer this tractor with a diesel. A three-point hitch with draft control and live hydraulics were standard, but power steering was an option.

The Farmall 404 was lighter and smaller than the Farmall 340, presumably to cut costs. Note that the 404 tested at almost five horsepower more than the 340 with the same engine. This indicates the variables that can occur in the tests.

Models and Variations

Model	Years Built
404 G	1961–1967
404 L	1961–1967

Specifications: Model 404 G

Engine: Four-cylinder
Fuel: Gasoline
Bore & stroke: 3.25x4.125 inches (82.55x104.78 mm)
Displacement: 134.8 ci (2,208 cc)
Engine speed: 2,000 rpm
Power: 36.7 PTO hp
Transmission: Eight speeds forward (with T/A; four-speed transmission with two-range auxiliary)
Weight: 6,645 pounds (3,014 kg)

Specifications: Model 404 L

Engine: Four-cylinder
Fuel: LPG
Bore & stroke: 3.25x4.125 inches (82.55x104.78 mm)
Displacement: 134.8 ci (2,208 cc)
Engine speed: 2,000 rpm
Power: Not tested
Transmission: Eight speeds forward with optional two-range auxiliary
Weight: Not tested

Serial Numbers: Model 404

Beginning S/N	Year
501	1961
810	1962
1936	1963
2180	1964
2531	1965
2754	1966
2941	1967

A fair fiesta!

The costume classes and dress-an-animal con[...]
dience members alike. This horse-sized pinata was pa[...]

The Great Stone[...]
Sept. 2-7   St[...]
[...] www.s[...]

...unty Fair
...0-16
...a, Ohio
...www.cuyfair.com

	19)
5:30 p.m.	4-H horse expo
6 p.m.	Elvis tribute
...p.m.	Sheep-to-shawl demonstration
	Junior fair bake-off and auction
	4-H dog agility demonstration
7:30 p.m.	Get Back (Beatles tribute band)

Saturday, Aug. 15

...m.	Horse show
	4-H showmanship sweepstakes
2 p.m.	Camp Rock Revisited (tribute bands to Demi Lovato, Hannah Montana and Jonas Brothers)
5:30 p.m.	Shameless (Garth Brooks tribute band)
7 p.m.	Pie eating contest, ages 5-19
	4-H market livestock auction
7:30 p.m.	The System (Bob Seger tribute band)

Sunday, Aug. 16

12:30 p.m.	4-H horse expo
3 p.m.	Demolition derby qualifier
7 p.m.	Demolition derby
9:30 p.m.	Fireworks

Guernsey County Fair

The 404 was all new when it came out in late 1960 as a 1961 model. This 1962 404 featured full hydrostatic steering with no mechanical connection between the front wheels and the steering wheel. Owners: Gary and Pat Keister, Patoka, Illinois

Chapter 2

Large Four-Cylinder Farmalls

The Farmall F-30, M, Super M,

Super M-TA, 400, 450, 504, 544

The Farmall F-30, 1931–1939

The Farmall Regular had revolutionized power farming, but farmers were clamoring for even more power. Tractor manufacturers responded to the call, producing the Case CC (1929), the Oliver Hart-Parr 18-27 (1930), and the Allis-Chalmers Row-Crop (1931). These were well-designed all-purpose tractors in the 30-belt-horsepower class. (The John Deere G, also in the 30-horsepower class, did not enter production until the model year 1937.) Thus, in 1931, International Harvester introduced the bigger, more powerful F-30. The designation "F-30" was meant to loosely stand for "Farmall, 30 horsepower." The next year, Harvester added the F-20, and the same connotation applied.

The F-30 was a scaled-up and improved version of the Regular. The longer, heavier tractor could plow almost an acre per hour with a three-bottom plow (the regular was rated for a two-bottom plow). The 284-ci (4,654-cc) engine was based on the successful McCormick 10-20 engine, which used the same 4.25x5-inch (108x127-mm) bore and stroke arrangement. Both were rated at 1,150 rpm, although early 10-20s were rated at slower engine speeds.

The F-30 featured steering and brakes similar to the Farmall Regular. Rather than being open to the elements, however, the F-30 steering gears were covered by a flat housing which acquired the nickname "duckbill." Power was transmitted through a four-speed gearbox and an all-gear final drive. Dual tricycle front wheels were standard, but Harvester released a narrow-tread version in 1932 and an adjustable wide-front in 1934. In the same year they introduced a high-crop version with a fixed-width front axle. Rubber tires became an option in 1934, too. With rubber tires from the factory came an optional higher-speed fourth gear. A worm-gear steering drive replaced the duckbill type in late 1934.

For the 1937 model year (starting in November 1936), International Harvester began to paint new Farmalls the famous Farmall Red rather than the old battleship gray. IH introduced a hydraulic power lift in 1938. Only about 28,000 F-30s were sold during the eight-year production run.

Models and Variations		Serial Numbers: Model F-30	
Model	Years Built	Beginning S/N	Year
F-30	1931–1939	501	1931
		1184	1932
Specifications: Model F-30		4305	1933
(tested on steel wheels)		5526	1934
Engine: Four-cylinder		7032	1935
Fuel: Kerosene		10407	1936
Bore & stroke: 4.25x5.0 inches		18684	1937
(107.95x127 mm)		27186	1938
Displacement: 283.7 ci (4,649 cc)		29007	1939
Engine speed: 1,150 rpm			
Power: 32.8 PTO hp			
Transmission: Four speeds forward			
Weight: 5,990 pounds (2,717 kg)			

The F-30 was longer and weighed over 1,000 pounds (454 kg) more than the F-20. Production began in 1931 and ended in 1939, although some were built from parts into 1940. This is a 1934 model.

The 1935 F-30 was considerably larger and more powerful than the original Farmall Regular. Its engine displaced 284 ci (4,654 cc) to the Regular's 221 ci (3,622 cc). Owner: John Wagner

Advertisement for the Farmall line of row-crop tractors

The F-30 was a true three-plow tractor designed to appeal to the farmer with more land to till. With the start of the 1937 model year, the tractors were painted the familiar Farmall Red.

The Farmall M, 1939–1952

The Farmall M was rated for three 14-inch plow bottoms.

The big M, an all-new tractor with attractive Raymond Loewy styling, replaced the F-30 in 1939. Unless seen together, it was difficult to tell the H from the M. The M was longer, taller, and more powerful. It also cost a staggering $200 more than the H (about the same price differential between a '39 Chevrolet and a Pontiac). The new 248-ci (4,064-cc) overhead-valve four provided enough power for three plow bottoms. Kerosene (or distillate) and gasoline versions were available.

Gone were the cable-operated steering brakes of the F-30. Brake pedals on the right side of the platform could be locked together for highway travel. A new five-speed transmission provided more flexibility than the F-30.

Also available, much to the surprise of the competition, was the diesel version, or MD. Caterpillar diesels had been at work on large farms since 1932. Harvester introduced its first diesel tractor, the WD-40 (not to be confused with today's popular lubricant) in 1934. The M and MD had the same engine block, but internally the diesel was much stronger with five instead of three main bearings. The compression ratio was increased 14:1. The MD diesel engine employed Harvester's unique all-weather starting system. The engine was designed to

Models and Variations

Model	Years Built
M	1939–1952
MD	1939–1952

Specifications: Model M
Engine: Four-cylinder
Fuel: Distillate
Bore & stroke: 3.875x5.25 inches
(98.43x133.35 mm)
Displacement: 247.7 ci (4,059 cc)
Engine speed: 1,450 rpm
Power: 34.16 PTO hp
Transmission: Five speeds forward
Weight: 6,770 pounds (3,071 kg)

Specifications: Model M
Engine: Four-cylinder
Fuel: Gasoline
Bore & stroke: 3.875x5.25 inches
(98.43x133.35 mm)
Displacement: 247.7 ci (4,059 cc)
Engine speed: 1,450 rpm
Power: 36.07 PTO hp
Transmission: Five speeds forward
Weight: 6,770 pounds (3,071 kg)

Rear tire size: 11.25x36

Specifications: Model MD
Engine: Four-cylinder
Fuel: Diesel
Bore & stroke: 3.875x5.25 inches
(98.43x133.35 mm)
Displacement: 247.7 ci (4,059 cc)
Engine speed: 1,450 rpm
Power: 35.02 PTO hp
Transmission: Five speeds forward
Weight: 7,570 pounds (3,434 kg)
Rear tire size: 12x38

Serial Numbers: Models M and MD

Beginning S/N	Year
501	1939
7240	1940
25371	1941
50988	1942
60011	1943
67424	1944
88085	1945
105564	1946
122823	1947
151708	1948
180514	1949
213579	1950
247518	1951
290923	1952

run as a spark-ignited gasoline engine. Thus the engine could be started on gasoline and switched over to diesel after it had warmed up. The driver used a lever near the platform to accomplish the switch over. When the lever was in the gasoline or starting position, ports in the combustion chambers were uncovered, lowering the compression ratio and exposing the spark plugs. The lever also activated the carburetor. Then, with the engine operating on gasoline, moving the lever to the diesel position closed the ports, shut off the carburetor and ignition, and activated the diesel fuel injectors. It then continued to run as a diesel. The system was complicated, but it worked well.

Options for the M included a Lift-All hydraulic implement lift. Dual narrow front wheels, or an adjustable wide front end were also options. High-crop versions were available with either wide fronts, or a single front wheel. Serial number prefixes were FBK for the M, FBKV for the MV (high-crop), FBDK for the MD, FBDKV for the diesel high-crop, etc.

The Model M was the also assembled in the new plant in Doncaster, England. Harvester released the British BM in 1949 and the BMD in 1952.

Above: *The M came out in 1939 with a brand-new four-cylinder OHV engine of 248 ci (4,064 cc). This is a 1949 model. Owner: Norm Sevcik*

Above, both photos: *Owners John and Mary Lou Poch of New Holstein, Wisconsin, collect steel-wheeled tractors. Although rubber tires were standard equipment in the 1940 model year, full steel was a popular option.*

This 1949 Farmall M ran on LPG fuel. IH did not offer the LPG in 1949, but it was a popular aftermarket conversion in the 1950s. Owner: John Wagner

From Marion County, Kansas, this yellow but essentially standard 1948 Farmall M wide-front was used for a variety of highway department duties. Owner: John Wagner, White Pigeon, Michigan

This M (serial number 1027) is the seventy-second one built at the Doncaster, England, plant. Doncaster Ms were later labeled "BM," signifying "Made-In-Britain."

The diesel-powered Farmall M came out in 1941. Although it cost 50 percent more than the gasoline version, fuel consumption was about 33 percent less. Owner: Alan Smith, McHenry, Illinois

1939 advertisement from the Country Gentleman

This wide-front-end 1949 version of the M is one of the 12,000 Ms made at International Harvester's Louisville plant. Owner John Wagner is pictured.

This single-front-wheel high-clearance version of the
Farmall M came from the cotton fields of the South.
This is a 1948 model.

The Farmall Super M, MD and M-TA, 1952–1954

The Super M was essentially the same tractor as the M, but an LPG (liquefied petroleum gas) option was added. All versions of the engine received a displacement increase from 248 ci (4,064 cc) to 264 ci (4,326 cc). Hydraulics became standard equipment.

In late 1953, Harvester introduced the Super M-TA for the 1954 model year, adding a live hydraulic system and moving the battery to a spot below the driver's seat. The T/A, or Torque Amplifier, was a power-shift planetary gearbox that gave a ratio increase of 1.482:1. This effectively gave the Super M-TA ten speeds forward and two in reverse. To change the ratio, the operator simply moved a lever with the left hand without having to de-clutch or change the throttle. Since the M-TA had maximum pulling power in the "low" ratio and would be the same as the regular Super M, the M-TA was not tested at the University of Nebraska.

Models and Variations

Model	Years Built
Super M	1952–1954

Specifications: Super M
Engine: Four-cylinder
Fuel: Gasoline
Bore & stroke: 4.0x5.25 inches
  (101.6x133.35 mm)
Displacement: 263.9 ci (4,325 cc)
Engine speed: 1,450 rpm
Power: 43.92 PTO hp
Transmission: Ten speeds forward
  (with T/A)
Weight: 8,929 pounds (4,050 kg)

Specifications: Super M
Engine: Four-cylinder
Fuel: LPG
Bore & stroke: 4.0x5.25 inches
  (101.6x133.35 mm)
Displacement: 263.9 ci (4,325 cc)
Engine speed: 1,450 rpm
Power: 45.66 PTO hp
Transmission: Ten speeds forward
  (with T/A)
Weight: 9,820 pounds (4,454 kg)

Specifications: Super M
Engine: Four-cylinder
Fuel: Diesel
Bore & stroke: 4.0x5.25 inches
  (101.6x133.35 mm)
Displacement: 263.9 ci (4,325 cc)
Engine speed: 1,450 rpm
Power: 46.73 PTO hp
Transmission: Ten speeds forward
  (with T/A)
Weight: 9,338 pounds (4,236 kg)

Rear tire size: 13x38

Serial Numbers: Super M

Beginning S/N	Year
501	1952
12516	1953
51977	1954

Farmall Super M-TA

60001	1954

Above: *In late 1952, the Farmall Super M replaced the regular M for model year 1953. This 1953 Super M was built in Louisville, Kentucky, and has an "L" serial number. Owner: Norval Poyser*

Left, both photos: *Actually made in 1952, this is the 347th Super M built. In University of Nebraska tests, the Super M had a horsepower of 44 on the belt at 1,450 rpm. Owner Dick Alberts, Kent City, Michigan, is pictured.*

IH of Great Britain produced fifty-three 1953 BMDs in gold livery to celebrate the coronation of HRH Queen Elizabeth II during that same year. Owner: John Pritchard

This 1958 British-built diesel tractor with the adjustable wide front end is virtually identical to the U.S. Super MD. Owner: Colin Shearn, Great Britain

This 1962 Made-in-Britain version of the Super MD used a glow-plug diesel, a different seat and fenders than the U.S. version, a three-point lift, and a differential lock. Owner: John Wagner

This 1954 Super M-TA is one of the "Super" letter series Farmalls that were only made in model years 1953 and 1954. They were immensely popular, but their short production period makes them quite collectable. Owner: Ron Hattendorf

This 1954 Farmall Super M-TA High Clearance tractor was one of only sixty-four made. High-clearance tractors were popular in sugar cane country. Owners: Gary and Pat Keister, Patoka, Illinois

The Super MD had almost one-third more power than the regular MD due mostly to a displacement increase from 247.7 ci (4,059 cc) to 263.9 ci (4,325 cc). Owner: Don Schaefer

The Farmall 400, 1954–1956

After only two model years, the Farmall 400 replaced the Super M. The 400 also only had a two-year production run, an indication of the competitive nature of the industry at that time.

The 400 was available with gasoline, diesel, or LPG engines. The engine was the same 264-ci (4,326-cc) four-cylinder unit offered on the Super M. All three fuel versions used the same block and had the same displacement.

International Harvester offered narrow- and wide-front row-crop versions, along with wide-front and single-front-wheel high-crop versions. The 400 featured same five-speed transmission with Torque Amplifier as the Super M. The Farmall Fast-Hitch with Hydra-Touch hydraulics completed the picture, and the Traction-Control feature was added in 1956.

Models and Variations

Model	Years Built
400	1954–1956

Specifications: Model 400

Engine: Four-cylinder
Fuel: Gasoline
Bore & stroke: 4.0x5.25 inches
 (101.6x133.35 mm)
Displacement: 263.9 ci (4,325 cc)
Engine speed: 1,450 rpm
Power: 48.7 PTO hp
Transmission: Ten speeds forward
 (with T/A)
Weight: 9,669 pounds (4,386 kg)
Rear tire size: 13x38

Serial Numbers: Model 400

Beginning S/N	Year
501	1954
4732	1955
29065	1956

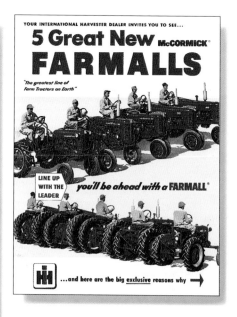

A 1950s brochure advertises the Farmall Cub, 100, 200, 300, and 400.

Made only in 1955 and 1956, this 1955 "Hi-Clear" 400 is extremely rare. A regular five-speed transmission, with the Torque Amplifier, gave ten speeds forward and two in reverse. Owner: Walter Keller

The Farmall 450, 1965–1958

The Farmall 450 was essentially a cosmetic update of the 400, except for an engine displacement increase from 264 to 281 ci (4,326 to 4,605 cc). This change placed the 450 in the over-50-horsepower class.

Models and Variations

Model	Years Built
450	1956–1958

Specifications: Model 450

Engine: Four-cylinder
Fuel: Gasoline
Bore & stroke: 4.125x5.25 inches
 (104.78x133.35 mm)
Displacement: 280.6 ci (4,598 cc)
Engine speed: 1,450 rpm
Power: 51.55 PTO hp
Transmission: Ten speeds forward
 (with T/A)
Weight: 8,905 pounds (4,039 kg)

Specifications: Model 450

Engine: Four-cylinder
Fuel: LPG
Bore & stroke: 4.125x5.25 inches
 (104.78x133.35 mm)
Displacement: 280.6 ci (4,598 cc)
Engine speed: 1,450 rpm
Power: 50.50 PTO hp
Transmission: Ten speeds forward
 (with T/A)
Weight: 9,071 pounds (4,115 kg)

Specifications: Model 450

Engine: Four-cylinder
Fuel: Diesel
Bore & stroke: 4.125x5.25 inches
 (104.78x133.35 mm)
Displacement: 280.6 ci (4,598 cc)
Engine speed: 1,450 rpm
Power: 48.78 PTO hp
Transmission: Ten speeds forward
 (with T/A)
Weight: 9,263 pounds (4,202 kg)

Rear tire size: 15.5x38

Serial Numbers: Model 450

Beginning S/N	Year
501	1956
1734	1957
21871	1958

With its 281-ci (4,605-cc) gas engine, the 1957 Farmall 450 was in the 50-horsepower class. LPG and diesel engines were also available with the same displacement. Owner: Marty Thieme, Noblesville, Indiana

Farmall 450s were made between 1956 and 1958. The 1958 diesel version, as shown, used a 281-ci (4,605-cc) International-built engine.

The Farmall 504, 1961–1968

Harvester released the all-new 1961 Farmalls in late 1960. The 504 featured new styling, fully hydrostatic power steering, and the Ferguson-type three-point hitch.

Gasoline, LPG, or diesel fuel options were offered. The first two engines displaced 152 ci (2,491 cc), while the diesel displaced 187 ci (3,064 cc). All were rated at 2,200 rpm. The 504 featured a five-speed transmission with the Torque Amplifier option. Narrow and wide front ends were options. From 1963 though the rest of the model run, a high-clearance version was available.

Models and Variations

Model	Years Built
504	1961–1968

Specifications: Model 504
Engine: Four-cylinder
Fuel: Gasoline
Bore & stroke: 3.375x4.25 inches
   (85.73x107.95 mm)
Displacement: 152.1 ci (2,492 cc)
Engine speed: 2,200 rpm
Power: 46.2 PTO hp
Transmission: Ten speeds forward
   (with T/A)
Weight: 7,870 pounds (3,570 kg)

Specifications: Model 504
Engine: Four-cylinder
Fuel: LPG
Bore & stroke: 3.375x4.25 inches
   (85.73x107.95 mm)
Displacement: 152.1 ci (2,492 cc)
Engine speed: 2,200 rpm
Power: 44.36 PTO hp
Transmission: Ten speeds forward
   (with T/A)
Weight: 7,895 pounds (3,581 kg)

Specifications: Model 504
Engine: Four-cylinder
Fuel: Diesel
Bore & stroke: 3.6875x4.39 inches
   (93.66x111.51 mm)
Displacement: 187.5 ci (3,073 cc)
Engine speed: 2,200 rpm
Power: 38.9 PTO hp
Transmission: Ten speeds forward
   (with T/A)
Weight: 8,075 pounds (3,663 kg)

Serial Numbers

Beginning S/N	Year
501	1961
810	1962
9000	1963
7732	1964
10697	1965
13596	1966
15113	1967
16115	1968

The 1962 Farmall 504 was offered in gasoline, LPG, or diesel versions. All were four-cylinder OHV types producing about 45 horsepower.

The 1968 Farmall 544 was Harvester's second model with hydrostatic drive. Four-cylinder gasoline or diesel engines were available. (Photo courtesy of State Historical Society of Wisconsin)

The Farmall 544, 1968–1973

The 544 replaced the 504 in 1968. The 544 featured either a manual five-speed with Torque Amplifier or a hydrostatic transmission with a manual two-range auxiliary. New dynamically balanced four-cylinder engines were both rated at 2,400 rpm. Harvester did not offer the LPG option. Other features included fully hydrostatic power steering, live hydraulics and PTO, and a Category II three-point hitch with draft control.

The 544 was one of the few IH tractors delivered to dealers with gold-painted hoods as a special sales promotion. These rare tractors are much sought after by collectors.

Models and Variations

Model	Years Built
544	1968–1973

Specifications: Model 544

Engine: Four-cylinder
Fuel: Gasoline
Bore & stroke: 3.8125x4.39 inches
   (96.84x111.51 mm)
Displacement: 200.3 ci (3,282 cc)
Engine speed: 2,200 rpm
Power: 52.84 PTO hp
Transmission: Ten speeds forward
   (with T/A)
Weight: 8,310 pounds (3769.42 kg)

Specifications: Model 544

Engine: Four-cylinder
Fuel: Diesel
Bore & stroke: 3.875x5.06 inches
   (98.43x128.52 mm)
Displacement: 238.7 ci (3,912 cc)
Engine speed: 2,200 rpm
Power: 52.95 PTO hp
Transmission: Ten speeds forward
   (with T/A)
Weight: 8,470 pounds (3,842 kg)

Specifications: Model 544

Engine: Four-cylinder
Fuel: Gasoline
Bore & stroke: 3.8125x4.39 inches
   (96.84x111.51 mm)
Displacement: 200.3 ci (3,282 cc)
Engine speed: 2,400 rpm
Power: 53.87 PTO hp
Transmission: Hydrostatic (with T/A)
Weight: 9,710 pounds (4,404 kg)

Serial Numbers: Model 544

Beginning S/N	Year
10253	1968
12541	1969
13585	1970
14507	1971
15262	1972
15738	1973

Chapter 3

Small Farmalls

The Farmall F-12, F-14, A, B, Super A, Super A-1,

100, 130, 140, C, Super C, 200, 230, 240, Cub

The Farmall F-12, 1932–1938

With a price tag half that for the F-20, the F-12 gave the small farmer all of the larger tractor's features and advantages except the power. The F-12, essentially a scaled-down version of the F-20/F-30 models, filled the bill for the myriad of farmers with forty to eighty acres, the farmer still working with horses, or the large-acreage farmer who needed a smaller chore tractor.

International Harvester introduced the F-12 in late 1932 with a Waukesha 113-ci (1,852-cc) engine. Although only 25 were built that year, production soon got rolling. At its peak in 1937, almost 36,000 were built. Total production eventually climbed to 123,000 units. In 1933, IH replaced the Waukesha engine with one of the same configuration they built themselves.

Capable of pulling one 16-inch (41-cm) bottom, the F-12 was also able to drive a 6-foot (1.83-m) mounted mower, a 10-foot (3-m) binder, and other equipment required by the small farmer or the truck gardener. Most Harvester-designed implements were made to operate with the optional hydraulic lift.

Production of the F-12 ended in 1938 when the F-14 replaced it. Variations on the F-12 included single front wheel, dual tricycle front end and adjustable wide front axle. Rubber tires were available from the start, but most early F-12s left the factory on steel. If ordered with rubber tires, a faster high gear could be provided in the three-speed transmission. In addition to the Farmall F-12, IH offered a Fairway version. Harvester also produced some standard-tread versions but they were not Farmalls.

An ad for the F-12 stressed the tractor's versatility.

Models and Variations

Model	Years Built
F-12	1932–1938

Specifications: Model F-12

Engine: Four-cylinder
Fuel: Gasoline
Bore & stroke: 3.0x4.0 inches
   (76.2x101.6 mm)
Displacement: 113.1 ci (1,853 cc)
Engine speed: 1,400 rpm
Power: 16.2 PTO hp
Transmission: Three speeds forward
Weight: 3,280 pounds (1,488 kg)

Specifications: Model F-12

Engine: Four-cylinder
Fuel: Kerosene
Bore & stroke: 3.0x4.0 inches
   (76.2x101.6 mm)
Displacement: 113.1 ci (1,853 cc)
Engine speed: 1,400 rpm
Power: 14.59 PTO hp
Transmission: Three speeds forward
Weight: 3,280 pounds (1,488 kg)

Rear tire size: 9.00x40

Serial Numbers: Model F-12

Beginning S/N	Year
501	1932
526	1933
4881	1934
17411	1935
48660	1936
81837	1937
117518	1938

The 1937 F-12 featured a four-cylinder engine of 113 ci (1,852 cc) operating at 1,400 rpm. It was available in dual-tricycle, wide-front, and single-front-wheel configurations.

The Farmall F-14, 1938–1939

The F-14 replaced the almost identical F-12 in 1938. The two tractors even shared the "FS" serial number prefix, but Harvester added a gap between the last F-12 (123942) and the first F-14 (124000). The only visual difference between the two models is that the steering wheel on the F-14 was raised about 8 inches and mounted on a standoff strut. The F-12 steering rod was parallel to the top of the hood, while that of the F-14 was at an angle. Standoff kits for the F-12 were available, however, since they placed the steering wheel at a much more comfortable angle for the driver. The other difference between the two is that the engine speed was increased on the F-14 from 1,400 rpm to 1,650 rpm, giving the F-14 14 percent more power, enough to pull a two-bottom 14-inch (36-cm) plow.

Models and Variations

Model	Years Built
F-14	1938–1939

Specifications: Model F-14

Engine: Four-cylinder
Fuel: Distillate
Bore & stroke: 3.0x4.0 inches
   (76.2x101.6 mm)
Displacement: 113.1 ci (1,853 cc)
Engine speed: 1,650 rpm
Power: 17 PTO hp
Transmission: Three speeds forward
Weight: 4,900 pounds (2,223 kg)

Rear tire size: 9.00x40

Serial Numbers: Model F-14

Beginning S/N	Year
124000	1938
139607	1939

(The last F-14 S/N was 155902)

Production of the F-14 began in 1938 when Harvester discontinued the F-12. The 1939 F-14 engine governor was set to 1,650 rpm, rather than 1,400 rpm as on the F-12. This gave the F-14 about a 9 percent horsepower advantage over the F-12.

The Farmall A, 1939–1947

The years 1938 to 1939 were a productive period for American tractor makers. Besides IH, Allis-Chalmers, Case, Deere, Ford, Massey, Minneapolis, and Oliver were big players with nicely styled and creditable tractors. IH was first in sales by a wide margin, and its newly styled line of tractors by Raymond Loewy seemed destined to keep them ahead of the competition. The first Loewy-styled tractor was the big red 1938 TD-18 crawler, but the Farmall Model A was soon to follow.

The Farmall A was a radical departure from previous tractors of any brand. Its most unusual feature was that the engine was offset to the left, while the operator's seat and steering wheel were offset to the right. The rear axle was longer on the left side than on the right. Loewy named this configuration "Culti-Vision." The Farmall A was only available in the wide-front configuration, but the front axle was high and long kingpins extended down to the front wheel hubs. Therefore the A was capable of cultivating taller crops. A high-crop version, the AV, featured larger wheels and tires, which increased the clearance by 6 inches (15.2 cm) for really tall crops. The A generally was equipped with a rear-mounted belt pulley and a rear PTO. The wheel spacing could be adjusted from 40 to 68 inches (101.6 to 172.7 cm).

The engine for the Farmall A was a 113-ci (1,852-cc) four-cylinder with overhead valves. Both gasoline and distillate versions were available. The gas version had a compression ratio of 6:1, while the distillate engine boasted 5:1. Initially, a thermosyphon cooling system was used but this was later switched to the water-pump variety. The A featured a four-speed transmission.

Models and Variations

Model	Years Built
A	1939–1947

Specifications: Model A

Engine: Four-cylinder
Fuel: Gasoline
Bore & stroke: 3.0x4.0 inches
  (76.2x101.6 mm)
Displacement: 113.1 ci (1,853 cc)
Engine speed: 1,400 rpm
Power: 16.86 PTO hp
Transmission: Four speeds forward
Weight: 3,570 pounds (1,619 kg)

Specifications: Model A

Engine: Four-cylinder
Fuel: Distillate
Bore & stroke: 3.0x4.0 inches
  (76.2x101.6 mm)
Displacement: 113.1 ci (1,853 cc)
Engine speed: 1,400 rpm
Power: 15.18 PTO hp
Transmission: Four speeds forward
Weight: 3,556 pounds (1,613 kg)

The 1941 Farmall A used essentially the same engine as the F-12 and F-14 Farmalls, but with improvements (such as a muffler). It was governed to 1,400 rpm.

The Farmall-AV
high-clearance tractor.

FARMALL-AV FOR HIGH CLEARANCE
Designed for Crops Grown on High Beds . . .

THE Farmall-AV is a high-clearance tractor designed for work in crops planted on high beds. It is especially adapted to crops such as asparagus and sugar cane, in which cultivation is continued until the plants have reached considerable height. It is powered with the same fine 4-cylinder engine as the Farmall-A and is in all respects the same tractor with modifications in design to give it 5½ extra inches of crop clearance. It is a Culti-Vision tractor.

One of the reasons why these small Farmalls have such a wide range of utility—why they are so well-adapted to row-crop requirements—is the number of machines built to hitch directly to them to make simple compact units that are easy to handle in any field or crop. These machines are all of the simplest design possible—consistent with the work they have to do—so that they can be made available at prices comparable with the price of horse drawn equipment. This is in line with Harvester's purpose to bring to the users of small tractors equipment that owners of larger tractors and equipment have enjoyed.

According to reliable figures, it takes from four to five acres of land to support one horse. Therefore, the man who keeps one to four horses has to figure that the crops from four to twenty acres of his farm have to be set aside to feed his horses or mules. If he is farming eighty acres and is keeping four work animals, he can

really only count on sixty acres of his eighty for his income crops. In other words, by substituting tractor for horse power he adds twenty productive acres to his farm.

The Farmall-AV has a crop clearance of nearly 27 inches.

6

Above: *A page from an early Farmall catalog touts the benefits of farming with the Farmall AV.*

Above, both photos: *A 1950 special high-crop version of the A provided extra clearance for taller garden crops, such as asparagus.*

Right: *The D320, built from 1956 to 1962, uses the IHC DD99 Neuss-built engine of 100 ci (1,631 cc) with a bore and stroke of 3.25x4 inches (82.6x101.6mm). It is rated at 20 hp at 1,900 rpm. Owner: Johann Hood.*

Left and above, both photos: *The 1950 FG, built in the German Neuss factory, was a modernized version of the Farmall F-12, roughly equivalent to the U.S. Farmall A. The four-cylinder engine displaced 125 ci (2,048 cc).*

The Farmall B, 1939–1947

The Farmall B and the Farmall A shared the same serial number sequence. They were, in fact, the same tractor except for the wheel arrangement. The B had two long rear axles with the engine in the middle. The driver still sat off to the right, however, as on the A. All of the B tractors were narrow front, either dual tricycle or single front wheel. Both the A and the B had a basic weight of around 2,000 pounds (907 kg). Both were nominally weighted with ballast that doubled the weight. Wheel spacing (rear) of from 64 to 92 inches (162.6 to 233.7 cm) was possible. The B was not available in a high-crop version.

Models and Variations

Model	Years Built
B	1939–1947

Specifications: Model B

Engine: Four-cylinder
Fuel: Gasoline
Bore & stroke: 3.0x4.0 inches
   (76.2x101.6 mm)
Displacement: 113.1 ci (1,853 cc)
Engine speed: 1,400 rpm
Power: 16.82 PTO hp
Transmission: Four speeds forward
Weight: 3,740 pounds (1,696 kg)

Rear tire size: 9.00x24

Serial Numbers: Models A and B

Beginning S/N	Year
501	1939
6744	1940
41500	1941
80739	1942
96390	1944
113218	1945
146700	1946
182964	1947

The Model B was the last of the Loewy-styled Farmalls to come out in 1939. This 1942 model used two long rear axles and had the engine in the center. Owner: Don Wolf, Ft. Wayne, Indiana

The Farmall Super A, 1947–1954

Models and Variations

Model	Years Built
Super A	1947–1954
Super A-1	1954

Specifications: Super A

Engine: Four-cylinder
Fuel: Gasoline
Bore & stroke: 3.0x4.0 inches
  (76.2x101.6 mm)
Displacement: 113.1 ci (1,853 cc)
Engine speed: 1,400/1,650 rpm
Power: Not tested
Transmission: Four speeds forward
Weight: Not tested

Specifications: Super A-1

Engine: Four-cylinder
Fuel: Gasoline
Bore & stroke: 3.125x4.0 inches
  (79.38x101.6 mm)
Displacement: 122.7 ci (2,011 cc)
Engine speed: 1,400 rpm
Power: Not tested
Transmission: Four speeds forward
Weight: Not tested

Rear tire size: 9.00x24
             7.50x32 (AV)

Serial Numbers: Super A

Beginning S/N	Year
250001	1947
250082	1948
268196	1949
281269	1950
300126	1951
324470	1952
336880	1953
353347	1954

The main feature of the Super A was the Touch-Control hydraulic implement lift system, which incorporated left and right lift cylinders. Splined rear axles improved adjustments to the rear wheel spacing once made by changing, or reversing, wheels and rims.

An electrical system, with starter, lights, battery, and generator, were standard equipment on the Super A. Also, most Super A

tractors were delivered with the governors set to 1,650 rpm, for a substantial power boost.

The A-1 version was the same as the Super A, but with the C-123 engine with 122.7-ci (2,011-cc) displacement. Governed speed was dropped back to the previous 1,400 rpm. The increased displacement and the reduced speed about cancelled each other out, so power remained the same.

The 1953 Super A was the same as the A with the addition of the Touch-Control hydraulic system.

The Farmall 100, 1954–1956

Although still much the same as the original Farmall A, the Model 100 featured a new grille and stainless steel hood numbers. The engine was the same as that used in the A-1 version, but Harvester increased the compression ratio from 6:1 to 6.5:1. The tractor now could handle two 14-inch (36-cm) plow bottoms in most soils.

Also new for the 100 was the Farmall Fast-Hitch. IH offered two hitch sizes: The Model 100s and 200s were equipped with the smaller of the two; the Model 300s and 400s had the larger. Bigger tractors could use the smaller implements, but not vice versa. Tractors with the Fast-Hitch also had Traction-Control, IH's response to Ferguson's Draft Control.

In addition to the above improvements, Harvester beefed up the steering, brakes, and power train. A high-crop version was available, but there were no front-end options.

Models and Variations

Model	Years Built
100	1954–1956

Specifications: Model 100

Engine: Four-cylinder
Fuel: Gasoline
Bore & stroke: 3.125x4 inches (79.38x101.6 mm)
Displacement: 122.7 ci (2,011 cc)
Engine speed: 1,400 rpm
Power: 18.34 PTO hp
Transmission: Four speeds forward
Weight: 4,338 pounds (1,968 kg)

Rear tire size: 11x24

Serial Numbers: Model 100

Beginning S/N	Year
501	1954
1720	1955
12895	1956

The 1955 Model 100 was a cosmetically updated version of the Model A-1. Mechanically the same, the 100 had the new grille and raised stainless lettering. Owner: Darius Harms

The Farmall 130, 1956–1957

Models and Variations

Model	Years Built
130	1956-1958

Specifications: Model 130

Engine: Four-cylinder
Fuel: Gasoline
Bore & stroke: 3.125x4 inches
   (79.38x101.6 mm)
Displacement: 122.7 ci (2,011 cc)
Engine speed: 1,400 rpm
Power: 21.38 PTO hp
Transmission: Four speeds forward
Weight: 4,615 pounds (2,093 kg)

Rear tire size: 11x24

Serial Numbers: Model 130

Beginning S/N	Year
501	1956
1120	1957
8363	1958

Although the basic tractor was the same as the Model 100, the Model 130 shared the white trim of its stable mates. Harvester also increased the compression ratio from 6.5:1 to 6.94:1. Engine speed remained the same. A high-clearance version was available.

The 1957 Farmall 130 was an upgrade of the Farmall 100, which superceded the Super A. The 130 was produced from 1956 through 1958. This one has a mounted one-bottom plow.

The Farmall 140, 1958–1975

New square-grille styling identified the Model 140. About the only technical change IH made was the switch to a 12-volt electrical system. A high-clearance version was available. The offset configuration remained popular with both Farmall and International (Industrial) 140s.

The 140 replaced the Farmall 130 in 1958. Maximum belt horsepower from the C-123 engine was increased to 21, and the four-speed transmission was retained. This is a 1962 model.

Models and Variations		Serial Numbers: Model 140	
Model	Years Built	Beginning S/N	Year
140	1958–1975	501	1958
		2011	1959
Specifications: Model 140		8082	1960
Engine: Four-cylinder		11168	1961
Fuel: Gasoline		16637	1962
Bore & stroke: 3.125x4 inches		21181	1963
(79.38x101.6 mm)		24716	1964
Displacement: 122.7 ci (2,011 cc)		27964	1965
Engine speed: 1,400 rpm		30775	1966
Power: 21.16 PTO hp		34325	1967
Transmission: Four speeds forward		36927	1968
Weight: 4,826 pounds (2,189 kg)		39514	1969
		43767	1970
Rear tire size: 11x24		44424	1971
		46605	1972
		48507	1973
		50720	1974
		54723	1975

This 1963 version of the popular 140 was used to cultivate taller vegetables such as asparagus. Like the other 140s, this Hi-Clear has a more comfortable wide-bench seat with a backrest.

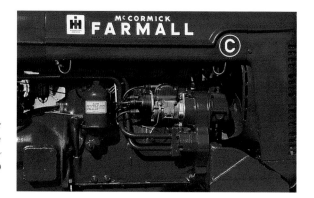

The C replaced the Model B in the IH lineup. An operator's platform puts the driver above the tractor rather than astride. This is a 1949 model.

The Farmall C, 1948–1951

The Farmall C replaced the Model B. It retained the same C-113 engine (governed at 1,650 rpm) and the same four-speed transmission. The C used straight axles with the transmission and differential beneath the platform. The B (and the A) featured an offset platform and operator seat with the transmission in a tunnel next to the operator. In the spirit of the old F-12 and F-14, the axle arrangement of the C included sliding hubs, making it easier to adjust the rear wheel treads. The drop box axles of the B meant the rear treads could only be adjusted by reversing the wheels.

   With the new raised platform, the seat was now on-center, giving the operator a view along both sides of the engine. The C was noted for its high steering-wheel angle. The

steering shaft ran along the left side of the engine through two universal joints

   The C looked bigger than the B it replaced because it had larger rear tires (9x36 instead of 8x24). The larger tires were necessary for the tractor to be level, but they also improved the traction.

   Harvester's Touch Control hydraulic system, which used an engine-driven pump, was an option on the C.

Models and Variations

Model	Years Built
C	1948–1951

Specifications: Model C

Engine: Four-cylinder
Fuel: Gasoline
Bore & stroke: 3x4 inches (76.2x101.6 mm)
Displacement: 113.1 ci (1,853 cc)
Engine speed: 1,650 rpm
Power: 19.91 PTO hp
Transmission: Four speeds forward
Weight: 4,409 pounds (2,000 kg)

Rear tire size: 9x36

Serial Numbers: Model C

Beginning S/N	Year
501	1948
22624	1949
47010	1950
71880	1951

In the early 1950s, IH launched a dramatic marketing program for its small tractor line, painting Cs, Cubs, and Super As a striking white. This is a 1950 Farmall C.

The Farmall Super C, 1951–1954

The Super C, an upgrade of the original C, featured new disk brakes and a larger-displacement engine, the C-123, which operated at 1,650 rpm. The hydraulic system, starter, and lights were standard equipment. Also new on the Super C was a variable-rate seat spring with a double-acting shock absorber.

For optional equipment, either a dual tricycle or an adjustable wide-front could be ordered, as well as a magneto ignition system. Later in the production run (1954) the Farmall Fast-Hitch made its debut on the Super C.

Models and Variations

Model	Years Built
Super C	1951–1954

Specifications: Model Super C

Engine: Four-cylinder
Fuel: Gasoline
Bore & stroke: 3.125x4 inches
    (79.38x101.6 mm)
Displacement: 122.7 ci (2,011 cc)
Engine speed: 1,650 rpm
Power: 22.92 PTO hp
Transmission: Four speeds forward
Weight: 5,041 pounds (2,287 kg)

Rear tire size: 10x36

Serial Numbers: Model Super C

Beginning S/N	Year
100001	1951
131157	1952
159130	1953
187788	1954

Above: *The 1951 Super C had a displacement increase over the plain C of 0.125 inches (3.175 mm), giving it a 15 percent power increase. Owner: Mary Lou Bunker-Langy*

Facing page: *The 1958 Super FCD (French-Model C-Diesel) was much the same as the American version. The French-built FD123 diesel displaced 123 ci (2,016 cc), the same as the gasoline engine in its U.S. counterpart. Owner: Sylvere Portier*

The Farmall 200, 1954–1956

The 200 got the new grille and raised stainless steel hood lettering of the three-numbered series. (Some early 200s were delivered with the old grille, however.) The engine received a compression ratio increase from 6:1 to 6.5:1 with special pistons and a hardened crankshaft. Otherwise, it was much the same as the Super C, including the 1,650 rpm governor setting.

Hydra-Creeper was an option on the 200. This feature was an add-on hydrostatic drive run by the PTO, which allowed the very slow movement needed to transplant certain vegetables.

Models and Variations

Model	Years Built
200	1954–1956

Specifications: Model 200

Engine: Four-cylinder
Fuel: Gasoline
Bore & stroke: 3.125x4 inches
    (79.38x101.6 mm)
Displacement: 122.7 ci (2,011 cc)
Engine speed: 1,650 rpm
Power: 22.09 PTO hp
Transmission: Four speeds forward
Weight: 5,331 pounds (2,418 kg)

Rear tire size: 10x36

Serial Numbers: Model 200

Beginning S/N	Year
501	1954
1032	1955
10904	1956

Successor to the Farmall Super C, the 200 came out in 1954. The 123-ci (2,016-cc) four-cylinder engine, turning at 1,650 rpm, gave the 200 a maximum belt horsepower of 24.11. This is a 1955 model.

The Farmall 230, 1956–1958

The Model 230 featured a compression ratio increased to 6.94:1 from the 200's 6.5:1. With the governor reset to 1,800 rpm, the 230 received a solid two-plow rating. Cosmetically, the 230 featured the white trim of others in this series, otherwise, it was much the same as the Model 200 it replaced.

Models and Variations

Model	Years Built
230	1956-1958

Specifications: Model 230

Engine: Four-cylinder
Fuel: Gasoline
Bore & stroke: 3.125x4 inches
 (79.38x101.6 mm)
Displacement: 122.7 ci (2,011 cc)
Engine speed: 1,800 rpm
Power: 24.28 PTO hp
Transmission: Four speeds forward
Weight: 5,330 pounds (2,418 kg)

Rear tire size: 10x36

Serial Numbers: Model 230

Beginning S/N	Year
501	1956
815	1957
6827	1958

The Farmall 240, 1958–1961

Although much the same under the skin as the 230, the Model 240 looked entirely new. The biggest change, besides the new square styling, was in the operator position and steering.

The operator position now reflected the influence of the successful Ford and Ferguson tractors, which pioneered the "utility" configuration. Although the Farmall 240 retained its row-crop identity, the operator now sat in front of the rear axle, straddling the transmission and drive line, rather than on top with a proper platform. Because hydraulics were now used to control implements, it was no longer necessary for the operator to sit to the rear in order to reach implement handles. The steering also reflected the Ford and Ferguson approach. The steering wheel shaft drove a worm (or ball) gear, which pulled or pushed a drag link connected to a pitman arm at the front axle. This produced a rather flat steering wheel (with respect to horizontal) that was characteristic of Ford tractors back to the original Fordson of 1917.

Under the hood, IH reset the 240's governor to 2,000 rpm and gave the tractor a 12-volt electrical system.

Models and Variations

Model	Years Built
240	1958–1961

Specifications: Model 240

Engine: Four-cylinder
Fuel: Gasoline
Bore & stroke: 3.125x4 inches
   (79.38x101.6 mm)
Displacement: 122.7 ci (2,011 cc)
Engine speed: 2,000 rpm
Power: 28.32 PTO hp
Transmission: Four speeds forward
Weight: 6,085 pounds (2,760 kg)

Rear tire size: 12.4x36

Serial Numbers: Model 240

Beginning S/N	Year
501	1958
1777	1959
3415	1960
3889	1961

The 240, built from 1958 through 1961, was a complete makeover of the previous model 230. This 1960 model featured a more modern look and had on-center steering and seat.

The Farmall Cub, 1947–1964

The Cub has many distinctions. It is the smallest Farmall. It is the only IH tractor with a side-valve engine. Its name broke with tradition. It had the longest production run of any tractor in the world. While production of the Farmall Cub ended in 1964, it continued to be produced as the International Cub through 1975. The Cub is one of the most sought-after collectable tractors. Its small size and usefulness endears it to estate owners who like to mow and gather firewood. The would-be farmer seated on his Cub mowing grass imagines himself in bib overalls and a straw hat atop a mighty Farmall MD. Perhaps there is a little "Walter Mitty" in all of us!

The Cub used a unique 59.5-ci (975-cc) side-valve engine (IH label C-60) and a three-speed transmission. It lived and died with this combination, although in 1950 the engine speed was increased from 1,600 rpm to 1,800 rpm.

The configuration of the Cub was like that of the Farmall A, that is, offset engine to the left, driver and steering wheel to the right. This configuration provided great clearance and an excellent view for crop cultivation. The adequate clearance also lent itself to underbelly mower mounting, an arrangement that does a better job on the lawn than a rear-mounted mower.

A vintage ad for the Farmall Cub

Right and facing page: *The Cub, which came out in 1948, was aimed at the under-forty-acre farmer. A four-cylinder L-head engine of 10 horsepower (60 ci / 983 cc) powered the Cub through a three-speed transmission.*

The Lo-Boy was a variation on the Cub theme. It stood 7 inches (17.8 cm) lower at the hood line and featured an underneath exhaust (rather than the above-hood exhaust of the regular Cub). Many International Cubs and Cub Lo-Boys, painted bright yellow, were acquired for highway mowing.

Like the rest of the models in the Farmall line, the Cub featured styling changes to the grille, lettering, and paint. The few options included wheel weights, a rear PTO that would accept a belt pulley, Touch Control hydraulics, and an electrical system. More than fourteen custom implements were ultimately available, including a one-arm front-end loader.

Models and Variations		Serial Numbers: Cub	
Model	Years Built	Beginning S/N	Year
Cub	1947–1964	501	1947
		11348	1948

Specifications: Cub

Engine: Four-cylinder
Fuel: Gasoline
Bore & stroke: 2.625x2.75 inches
 (67.36x69.85 mm)
Displacement: 59.5 ci (975 cc)
Engine speed: 1,600 rpm
Power: 9.23 PTO hp
Transmission: Three speeds forward
Weight: 2,707 pounds (1,228 kg)

Specifications: Cub

Engine: Four-cylinder
Fuel: Gasoline
Bore & stroke: 2.625x2.75 inches
 (67.36x69.85 mm)
Displacement: 59.5 ci (975 cc)
Engine speed: 1,800 rpm
Power: 10.39 PTO hp
Transmission: Three speeds forward
Weight: 2,891 pounds (1,311 kg)

Rear tire size: 8x24 or 9x24 (also Lo-Boy)

Beginning S/N	Year
57831	1949
99536	1950
121454	1951
144455	1952
162285	1953
79412	1954
186441	1955
193658	1956
198231	1957
204389	1958
211441	1959
214974	1960
217382	1961
220038	1962
221383	1963
223453	1964
225110	1965

Farmall Cubs were made through 1964 in the regular and Lo-Boy configurations. This is a 1958 model. Owner: Mike Thompson, Genoa, Illinois

Above: *The Cub in white livery was startling to viewers on showroom floors across America in 1950. It was designed to attract attention to the entire Farmall lineup.*

Left: *The 1958 French Farmall Cub was manufactured at the Cima, Paris, factory. It has a fourcylinder engine of 60 ci (983 cc). Owner: Jean Faydi, Cahors, France*

Chapter 4

Six-Cylinder Farmalls Under 90 Horsepower

The Farmall 460, 560, 706, 656, 756,

766, 666, and Hydro 70

The Farmall 460, 1958–1963

The 460 was an over-50-horsepower tractor, rated for four plow bottoms. Available in gasoline, diesel, or LPG versions, the 460 featured dual-narrow-front, adjustable-wide-front, or high-clearance wide-front configurations.

The diesel version had a D-236 six-cylinder IH engine with glow-plug starting. Gone was the old switchover starting method pioneered by International. The gasoline and LPG models had C-221 six-cylinder engines. IH established this system of engine identifiers. The C or D letter indicated spark ignition or diesel. The numbers indicated displacement in cubic inches.

The 460 was equipped with a steering shaft assembly (with universal joints) that ran down from the instrument panel to the frame, then forward to a steering gearbox. This system supplanted the over-the-engine steering used on previous models. Power-assisted steering was standard.

Besides the bold new styling, the 460 featured an internal hydraulic pump, a proper instrument panel, a seat with a backrest, and a 12-volt electrical system (albeit with a generator, rather than an alternator). A five-speed transmission and Torque Amplifier was standard.

Early in the production run, farmers experienced final-drive failures with the 460. The new six-cylinder engine was over-taxing the final drive, which had originally been developed for the Farmall 400 and 450. It took about a year for IH to fix the problem. Although tractors were retrofitted with the new gears and shafts, the debacle had substantially damaged the company's reputation. Nevertheless, more than 43,000 Farmall 460s left the factory and, after the fix, gave excellent service.

The 460 was produced from 1958 through 1963. This 1963 model was equipped with a six-cylinder engine with 221 ci (3,622 cc) for the gasoline and LPG versions and 236 ci (3,867 cc) for the diesel.

Models and Variations		Serial Numbers: Model 460	
Model	Years Built	Beginning S/N	Year
460	1958–1963	501	1958
		4766	1959
Specifications: Model 460		16900	1960
Engine: Six-cylinder		22622	1961
Fuel: Gasoline		28029	1962
Bore & stroke: 3.56x3.69 inches		31552	1963

Specifications: Model 460

Engine: Six-cylinder
Fuel: Gasoline
Bore & stroke: 3.56x3.69 inches
   (90.424x93.73 mm)
Displacement: 221 ci (3,622 cc)
Engine speed: 1,800 rpm
Power: 46.94 PTO hp
Transmission: Ten speeds forward
   (with T/A)
Weight: 8,931 pounds (4,051 kg)

Rear tire size: 13.6x38

The Farmall 560, 1958–1963

The Farmall 560 made its debut on July 18, 1958. The first of the six-cylinder Farmalls, it came with gasoline, LPG, or diesel engines. This is a 1960 model.

The Farmall 560 was like a big brother to the 460. It was in the 60-horsepower class. It was the top of the line of IH row-crop tractors, supplanting the Farmall 450. With the exception of having some final-drive-line components designed to the same standards, the 560 had almost nothing in common with the 450. The big power increase soon led to breakages similar to those of the 460. IH was guilty of undue optimism in expecting these gears and shafts to stand up and of insufficient testing before production began. However, in an attempt to recover, IH made a heroic effort to develop a solution and retrofit existing tractors. The mistake cost IH much of its customer loyalty, and arch-rival Deere took over sales leadership.

The 560 and its smaller sibling the 460 were some of the handsomest tractors ever produced. The all-new styling featured long, powerful hoods covering smooth-running six-cylinder engines. In addition to the new styling, the 560 featured an internal hydraulic pump, a proper instrument panel, a seat with a backrest, and a 12-volt electrical system (with a generator instead of an alternator). Gasoline, LPG, or diesel versions were available. The traditional five-speed transmission with Torque Amplifier power-shift auxiliary was standard. The diesel version featured the D-282 six-cylinder IH engine. Glow-plug starting replaced the old switchover starting method. The gasoline and LPG engines were C-263 sixes.

A new system supplanted the over-the-engine steering used on earlier models. On the 560, a steering shaft assembly (with universal joints) ran down from the instrument panel to the frame, then forward to a worm-gear steering box. Power-assisted steering was standard.

Models and Variations

Model	Years Built
560	1958–1963

Specifications: Model 560

Engine: Six-cylinder
Fuel: Gasoline
Bore & stroke: 3.56x4.391 inches
  (90.42x111.53 mm)
Displacement: 263 ci (4,310 cc)
Engine speed: 1,800 rpm
Power: 61.04 PTO hp
Transmission: Ten speeds forward
  (with T/A)
Weight: 9,239 pounds (4,191 kg)

Specifications: Model 560

Engine: Six-cylinder
Fuel: LPG
Bore & stroke: 3.56x4.391 inches
  (90.42x111.53 mm)
Displacement: 263 ci (4,310 cc)
Engine speed: 1,800 rpm
Power: 57.06 PTO hp
Transmission: Ten speeds forward
  (with T/A)
Weight: 9,361 pounds

Specifications: Model 560

Engine: Six-cylinder
Fuel: Diesel
Bore & stroke: 3.69x4.391 inches
  (93.73x111.53 mm)
Displacement: 281.3 ci (4,610 cc)
Engine speed: 1,800 rpm
Power: 61.23 PTO hp
Transmission: Ten speeds forward
  (with T/A)
Weight: 11,245 pounds (5,101 kg)

Rear tire size: 15.5x38

Serial Numbers: Model 560

Beginning S/N	Year
501	1958
7341	1959
26914	1960
36125	1961
47798	1962
60278	1963

The 1961 Farmall 560 shown here was a Brass Tacks Demonstrator. A special package of decals, either factory or dealer installed, pointed out the features of the new tractor. Owner: Wilson Gatewood

The Farmall 706, 1963–1967

The "06" series of tractors actually began with the International 606 Utility tractor, an upgraded I-460, introduced in 1961. The 706, and its big brother the 806, however, were "clean-sheet-of-paper" designs. They were IH's answer to Deere's very successful New Generation line.

The Farmall 706 featured a central hydraulic system with three circuits—one for completely hydrostatic steering, a second for power brakes, and a third for implement control.

Three new six-cylinder engines were available in gasoline, LPG, and diesel. The LPG engine was the same as the gasoline version, but with a higher compression ratio. Originally the gasoline and LPG engines displaced 263 ci (4,310 cc) and the diesel 282 ci (4,621 cc). In November 1966, IH increased the displacement of the gas and LPG engines to 291 ci (4,769 cc) by increasing the bore diameter by 0.1875 inches (0.63 cm). This version did not have a higher compression ratio for LPG fuel. The diesel version, which displaced 310 ci (5,080 cc), used a new German-designed engine that featured direct injection instead of the glow plugs of the original engine.

A high-clearance option could be ordered, as well as an all-wheel-drive front end. The transmission consisted of a four-speed manual box and a two-range auxiliary with two control levers on the right side of the cowl. The optional Torque Amplifier, with a control on the left side of the cowl, provided sixteen forward speeds.

The 706 was produced from 1963 through 1967. The original six-cylinder gasoline and LPG engine used from 1963 to 1966 (this is a 1966 model) displaced 263 ci (4,310 cc) and gave a maximum belt horsepower of 74. Owner: Aaron Woker

Models and Variations

Model	Years Built
706 Early	1963–1966
706 Late	1967

Specifications: Model 706 Early

Engine: Six-cylinder
Fuel: Gasoline
Bore & stroke: 3.56x4.39 inches
  (90.42x111.53 mm)
Displacement: 263 ci (4,310 cc)
Engine speed: 2,300 rpm
Power: 73.82 PTO hp
Transmission: Sixteen speeds forward
  (with T/A)
Weight: 9,895 pounds (4,488 kg)

Specifications: Model 706 Early

Engine: Six-cylinder
Fuel: LPG
Bore & stroke: 3.56x4.39 inches
  (90.42x111.53 mm)
Displacement: 263 ci (4,310 cc)
Engine speed: 2,300 rpm
Power: 73.66 PTO hp
Transmission: Sixteen speeds forward
  (with T/A)
Weight: 9,953 pounds (4,515 kg)

Specifications: Model 706 Early

Engine: Six-cylinder
Fuel: Diesel
Bore & stroke: 3.69x4.39 inches
  (93.73x111.53 mm)
Displacement: 282 ci (4,621 cc)
Engine speed: 2,300 rpm
Power: 72.42 PTO hp
Transmission: Sixteen speeds forward
  (with T/A)
Weight: 10,011 pounds (4,541 kg)

Specifications: Model 706 Late

Engine: Six-cylinder
Fuel: Gasoline
Bore & stroke: 3.75x4.39 inches
  (95.25x111.51 mm)
Displacement: 290.8 ci (4,765 cc)
Engine speed: 2,300 rpm
Power: 76.56 PTO hp
Transmission: Sixteen speeds forward
  (with T/A)
Weight: 10,230 pounds (4,640 kg)

Specifications: Model 706 Late

Engine: Six-cylinder
Fuel: LPG
Bore & stroke: 3.75x4.39 inches
  (95.25x111.51 mm)
Displacement: 290.8 ci (4,765 cc)
Engine speed: 2,300 rpm
Power: 76.30 PTO hp
Transmission: Sixteen speeds forward
  (with T/A)
Weight: 10,410 pounds (4,722 kg)

Specifications: Model 706 Late

Engine: Six-cylinder
Fuel: Diesel
Bore & stroke: 3.88x4.38 inches
  (98.55x111.25 mm)
Displacement: 309.6 ci (5,073 cc)
Engine speed: 2,300 rpm
Power: 76.09 PTO hp
Transmission: Sixteen speeds forward
  (with T/A)
Weight: 10,710 pounds (4,858 kg)

Rear tire size: 15.5x38

Serial Numbers: Model 706

Beginning S/N	Year
501	1963
7073	1964
21162	1965
30288	1966
38521	1967

The 1963 Farmall 706 was very popular with farmers, and more than 52,000 were delivered. This diesel version has two batteries, two PTO outputs, and a three-point hitch. Owner: Don Schaefer

The Farmall 656, 1966–1972

The Farmall 656 did not replace the 706, but did replace the International 606. The 656 was available as either a Farmall or an International with the choice of a gasoline or diesel fuel system in row-crop or high-clearance versions.

The 656 was the first Farmall to be available with a hydrostatic transmission coupled with a two-range sliding-gear auxiliary. This option provided full-throttle speeds of from 0 to 21 mph (0 kph to 33.8 kph). The non-hydrostatic version used the traditional five-speed gearbox with the Torque Amplifier.

Like several other 1970 IH demonstrator tractors, some Farmall 656s were painted a special gold for promotional purposes.

Models and Variations

Model	Years Built
656	1966–1972

Specifications: Model 656

Engine: Six-cylinder
Fuel: Gasoline
Bore & stroke: 3.56x4.39 inches
  (90.42x111.53 mm)
Displacement: 262.5 ci (4,302 cc)
Engine speed: 1,800 rpm
Power: 63.85 PTO hp
Transmission: Ten speeds forward
  (with T/A)
Weight: 9,165 pounds (4,157 kg)
Rear tire size: 15.5x38

Specifications: Model 656

Engine: Six-cylinder
Fuel: Diesel
Bore & stroke: 3.69x4.39 inches
  (93.73x111.53 mm)
Displacement: 281.3 ci (4,610 cc)
Engine speed: 1,800 rpm
Power: 61.52 PTO hp
Transmission: Ten speeds forward (with
  T/A)
Weight: 9,235 pounds (4,189 kg)
Rear tire size: 15.5x38

Specifications: Model 656

Engine: Six-cylinder
Fuel: Gasoline
Bore & stroke: 3.56x4.39 inches
  (90.42x111.53 mm)
Displacement: 262.5 ci (4,302 cc)
Engine speed: 2,300 rpm
Power: 65.8 PTO hp
Transmission: Hydrostatic (with two-
  speed sliding-gear auxiliary)
Weight: 9,995 pounds (4,534 kg)
Rear tire size: 14.9x38

Specifications: Model 656

Engine: Six-cylinder
Fuel: Diesel
Bore & stroke: 3.69x4.39 inches
  (93.73x111.53 mm)
Displacement: 281.3 ci (4,610 cc)
Engine speed: 2,300 rpm
Power: 62.18 PTO hp
Transmission: Hydrostatic (with two-
  speed sliding-gear auxiliary)
Weight: 10,010 pounds (4,541 kg)
Rear tire size: 14.9x38

Serial Numbers: Model 656

Beginning S/N	Year
15505	1966
24372	1967
32007	1968
38861	1969
45384	1970
45497	1971
47951	1972

Above: *The 1971 Farmall 656 was available in gasoline or diesel versions. Both engines were six-cylinder types. The diesel displaced 281 ci (4,605 cc), while the gasoline version displaced 263 ci (4,310 cc). Owners: Neil and Clell Michel*

Left: *The 1967 Farmall 656 Hydro was the first hydrostatic-drive tractor available to the farmer. Owner: Ralph Kurtz, New Haven, Indiana*

The Farmall 756, 1967–1971

The Farmall 756 was internally much the same tractor as the 706 it replaced, but Harvester restyled it to match others in the 56 Series and improved the shift pattern. Since there were no major changes to the mechanics, no Nebraska tests were performed. The 756 was available in high-clearance or row-crop versions.

Between 1970 and 1971, IH produced a version called the 756 Custom at a reduced price. The tractor's relatively short production run makes it quite rare. The Custom featured single headlights in each fender, a smaller fuel tank, a single remote hydraulic control, and a smaller air filter. The Torque Amplifier was, however, standard equipment.

The 1969 Farmall 756 was a restyled version of the 706, offered in row-crop and high-clearance configurations. Owner: Paul Amstutz, Woodburn, Indiana

Models and Variations

Model	Years Built
756	1967–1971

Specifications: Model 756

Not tested
Rear tire size: 15.5x38

Serial Numbers: Model 756

Beginning S/N	Year
7501	1967
9940	1968
14125	1969
18356	1970
18374	1971

The Farmall 766, 1971–1975

In the fall of 1971, Harvester replaced the 56 Series with the 66 line. Thus, the Farmall 766 replaced the 756.

A 291-ci (4,769-cc) gasoline engine and a 360-ci (5,899-cc) diesel moved the 766 to the 80-horsepower class. While it retained the same basic configuration as the 756, the 766 featured a considerably beefed-up frame and front end.

An adjustable-wide-front axle had become standard equipment, although the tricycle version was still an option. The gasoline Farmall 766 appears to be the last tricycle tractor tested at Nebraska. Other options included a deluxe cab, an electrically actuated traction lock, and front wheel assist.

The eight-speed sliding-gear transmission was standard with the T/A as an optional add-on.

The 766 was offered from 1971 to 1975 and was available in either gasoline (291 ci/4,769 cc) or diesel (360 ci/5,899 cc) versions, both producing about 83 PTO horsepower. This is a 1974 model.

Models and Variations

Model	Years Built
766	1971–1975

Specifications: Model 766

Engine: Six-cylinder
Fuel: Gasoline
Bore & stroke: 3.75x4.39 inches
   (95.25x111.51 mm)
Displacement: 290.6 ci (4,762 cc)
Engine speed: 2,400 rpm
Power: 79.73 PTO hp
Transmission: Sixteen speeds forward
   (with T/A)
Weight: 11,880 pounds (5,389 kg)

Specifications: Model 766

Engine: Six-cylinder
Fuel: Diesel
Bore & stroke: 3.88x5.06 inches
   (98.55x128.52 mm)
Displacement: 359.8 ci (5,896 cc)
Engine speed: 2,400 rpm
Power: 85.45 PTO hp
Transmission: Sixteen speeds forward
   (with T/A)
Weight: 12,720 pounds (5,770 kg)

Rear tire size: 18.4x34

Serial Numbers: Model 766

Beginning S/N	Year
7101	1971
7416	1972
9611	1973
12378	1974
14360	1975

The Farmall 666, 1972–1975

Models and Variations

Model	Years Built
666	1972–1975

Specifications: Model 666

Engine: Six-cylinder
Fuel: Gasoline
Bore & stroke: 3.75x4.39 inches
(95.25x111.51 mm)
Displacement: 290.6 ci (4,762 cc)
Engine speed: 2,000 rpm
Power: 66.3 PTO hp
Transmission: Ten speeds forward
(with T/A)
Weight: 10,050 pounds (4,559 kg)

Rear tire size: 18.4x34

Serial Numbers: Model 666

Beginning S/N	Year
7500	1972
8200	1973
11585	1974
13131	1975

International Harvester did not replace the 656 in 1971 when it replaced the other 56 tractors, but held it over until 1972. The 666 was the smallest Farmall offered, producing around 70 horsepower with a drawbar pull of about 8,000 pounds (3,629 kg).

Harvester offered a 312-ci (5,113-cc) diesel or a 291-ci (4,769-cc) gasoline engine. The transmission was the regular five-speed unit with the optional Torque Amplifier. Hydrostatic power steering was standard.

Options abounded, including a sun shield that mounted to the roll bar, a narrow front, a choice of a two- or three-point hitch, and a high-clearance model. Until 1973, customers could order the 666 with a hydrostatic transmission, although this version was not tested at the University of Nebraska.

The 1973 Farmall 666 was available in either a gasoline or diesel engine version. Both engines were six-cylinder types, producing about 70 PTO horsepower. Owner: Kevin Wolken

The Farmall Hydro 70, 1973–1974

The Farmall Hydro 70 was simply a relabeled 666. Harvester changed the name to avoid direct comparisons between the two transmission types. Hydrostatic transmissions are by nature less efficient than gear drives and therefore have less pulling power. But, as some farmers saw it, the hydrostatic offered flexibility that more than made up for the loss in power, but still there was resistance to paying more for a tractor that pulled less.

Models and Variations

Model	Years Built
Hydro 70	1973–1974

Specifications: Hydro 70

Engine: Six-cylinder
Fuel: Gasoline
Bore & stroke: 3.75x4.39 inches
  (95.25x111.51 mm)
Displacement: 290.6 ci (4,762 cc)
Engine speed: 2,400 rpm
Power: 69.61 PTO hp
Transmission: Hydro (with two-speed
  sliding-gear auxiliary)
Weight: 10,140 pounds (4,600 kg)

Specifications: Hydro 70

Engine: Six-cylinder
Fuel: Diesel
Bore & stroke: 3.88x4.41 inches
  (98.55x112 mm)
Displacement: 312 ci (5,113 cc)
Engine speed: 2,400 rpm
Power: 69.51 PTO hp
Transmission: Hydro (with two-speed
  sliding-gear auxiliary)
Weight: 10,430 pounds (4,731 kg)

Rear tire size: 18.4x34

Serial Numbers: Hydro 70

Beginning S/N	Year
7501	1973
7570	1974

Chapter 5
Six-Cylinder Farmalls 90 to 100 Horsepower
The Farmall 806, 856, 826, and 966

The Farmall 806, 1963–1967

Billed as "the world's most powerful tricycle tractor," the 806 was available with a diesel, gasoline, or LPG engine. The release of the 806, arguably the world's best tractor in 1963, breathed new life into IH's farm tractor operation, which had been on life support. The 806 was all-new from the ground up, and it had sufficient testing to be mostly trouble free from the outset. When it appeared in 1963, its chief competition was the John Deere 4010, which had been out for two years. The 806 countered and trumped all of the 4010's advantages, and in 1964, Deere introduced the improved 4020.

The big news for the 806 (and the Deere 4010) was the central hydraulic system. Whereas the IH version had three separate circuits for the steering, brakes, and implement lift, the Deere system had a single circuit. IH engineers reasoned that multiple circuits would be a lot safer, should one "blow a hose."

The new diesel was the star, and it was the biggest seller by far. It featured direct injection and displaced 361 ci (5,916 cc) and boasted 94.93 horsepower during its Nebraska test. The gasoline and LPG engines displaced 301 ci (4,932 cc). All were six-cylinder units that produced about the same amount of power. An interesting innovation on the diesel was an ether cold-weather starting system in which a replaceable can of ether, triggered by a cable, directed a blast of ether into the intake manifold. Later, because of problems with the cable, a solenoid valve was used instead.

Two levers on the right side of the steering tower controlled the transmission. The inner lever selected high or low range (along with neutral and reverse), while the outer lever selected speeds in the four-speed gearbox. Thus, eight speeds forward were available. The optional Torque Amplifier lever was on the left side, and it doubled the available ratios.

The Farmall 806 came in tricycle- or wide-front versions with either a three-point hitch, or the Fast-Hitch. IH also offered a high-clearance version and factory front wheel assist (FWA). And, in 1965, it introduced a factory cab.

Facing page: The 1967 806 recorded almost 95 horsepower in its Nebraska test. Its six-cylinder diesel displaced 361 ci (5,916 cc). Gas and LPG versions of 301 ci (4,932 cc) were also available. Owner: Bruce Copper

Models and Variations

Model	Years Built
806	1963–1967

Specifications: Model 806

Engine: Six-cylinder
Fuel: Diesel
Bore & stroke: 4.125x4.5 inches (105x114 mm)
Displacement: 361 ci (5,916 cc)
Engine speed: 2,400 rpm
Power: 94.93 PTO hp
Transmission: Sixteen speeds forward (with T/A)
Weight: 11,895 pounds (5,396 kg)

Specifications: Model 806

Engine: Six-cylinder
Fuel: Gasoline
Bore & stroke: 3.813x4.391 inches (96.85x111.53 mm)
Displacement: 301 ci (4,932 cc)
Engine speed: 2,400 rpm
Power: 93.27 PTO hp
Transmission: Sixteen speeds forward (with T/A)
Weight: 11,045 pounds (5,010 kg)

Specifications: Model 806

Engine: Six-cylinder
Fuel: LPG
Bore & stroke: 3.813x4.391 inches (96.85x111.53 mm)
Displacement: 301 ci (4,932 cc)
Engine speed: 2,400 rpm
Power: 93.42 PTO hp
Transmission: Sixteen speeds forward (with T/A)
Weight: 11,525 pounds (5,228 kg)

Rear tire size: 18.4x34

Serial Numbers: Model 806

Beginning S/N	Year
501	1963
4709	1964
15946	1965
24038	1966

The 1965 806 was available in gasoline, LPG, and diesel versions. The diesel, by far the most popular, was German-built and featured direct injection. Owner: Ed Engen, Brodhead, Wisconsin

Built from 1963 to 1967, the 806, at 95 horsepower, was billed as the world's most powerful row-crop tractor.

Models and Variations

Model	Years Built
856	1967–1971

Specifications: Model 856

Engine: Six-cylinder
Fuel: Diesel
Bore & stroke: 4.312x4.625 inches
  (109.52x117.48 mm)
Displacement: 407 ci (6,670 cc)
Engine speed: 2,400 rpm
Power: 100 PTO hp
Transmission: Sixteen speeds forward
  (withT/A)
Weight: 14,875 pounds (6,747 kg)

Rear tire size: 18.4x38

Serial Numbers: Model 856

Beginning S/N	Year
7501	1967
9854	1968
19554	1969
32099	1970
32420	1971

The Farmall 856, 1967–1971

The 856 replaced the 806 in the Farmall lineup in 1967. It was restyled to match the others in the 56 Series and beefed up to handle the increased power of the enlarged six-cylinder diesel of 406.9 ci (6,668 cc). The 856 was the first naturally aspirated Farmall to exceed 100 horsepower during its Nebraska test.

Besides the engine change, the 856 incorporated the new IH "wedge-lock" design rear wheels, a system that made it much easier to change wheel tread widths. For the sake of convenience, IH began to use "spin-off" fuel filters. Engineers also changed the straight-line shift pattern of the range shifter on the 806 to an "H" pattern on the 856. This eliminated the need to go through low range when shifting from reverse to high, speeded the process, and alleviated a lot of gear grinding.

Comfort and convenience were fast becoming major selling factors in tractors. Realizing this, Harvester included an optional tilting steering wheel and a new hydraulic power seat on the 856. Equipped with folding armrests, the seat tilted, moved up or down, and slid back and forth. An improved factory cab with two doors was available in 1970. Without the cab, a factory ROPS (Roll-Over Protection System) was installed on the 856.

The 856 was available in regular row-crop (narrow and wide front) and in a high-clearance version. Gasoline and LPG versions were not available.

The 856 Custom was similar to the regular 856, but it was the stripped-down economy version. The Custom had a single remote hydraulic valve, single headlights in the fenders, a smaller fuel tank, and a smaller air filter.

The Farmall 856 replaced the 806 in 1967. It was restyled to bring it up-to-date, and it had a new, larger-displacement six-cylinder engine of 406.9 ci (6,669 cc). This is a 1969 model.

The Farmall 826, 1969–1971

The 800 Series Farmalls had rapidly grown to exceed 100 horsepower. The 700 Series remained around 75 horsepower, so in 1969, IH added the 826 to fill the 90 horsepower gap originally occupied by the venerable 806. A new German-built diesel of 358 ci (5,867 cc) replaced the old glow-plug 361-ci (5,916-cc) unit. The gasoline engine of 301 ci (4,932 cc) remained, however the gasoline option was no longer very popular.

IH offered two transmission options: an eight-speed sliding-gear manual with partial-range power shift (Torque Amplifier), or the fully hydrostatic stepless transmission with a two-speed sliding-gear auxiliary.

Standard equipment for the 826 included a Category II three-point hitch, power steering, and power brakes. High-clearance versions were available.

The Farmall 826 was one of several offered as Golden Demonstrator tractors in 1970. These tractors featured gold-painted sheet metal to draw attention to the IH line. Today, these gold models are very popular with collectors.

Models and Variations

Model	Years Built
826	1969–1971

Specifications: Model 826

Engine: Six-cylinder
Fuel: Gasoline
Bore & stroke: 3.813x4.391 inches
  (96.85x111.53 mm)
Displacement: 301 ci (4,932 cc)
Engine speed: 2,400 rpm
Power: 93.27 PTO hp
Transmission: Sixteen speeds forward
  (with T/A)
Weight: 11,895 pounds (5,396 kg)

Specifications: Model 826

Engine: Six-cylinder
Fuel: Diesel
Bore & stroke: 3.875x5.06 inches
  (98.43x128.52 mm)
Displacement: 358 ci (5,867 cc)
Engine speed: 2,400 rpm
Power: 92.19 PTO hp
Transmission: Sixteen speeds forward
  (with T/A)
Weight: 13,840 pounds (6,278 kg)

Specifications: Model 826

Engine: Six-cylinder
Fuel: Diesel
Bore & stroke: 3.875x5.06 inches
  (98.43x128.52 mm)
Displacement: 358 ci (5,867 cc)
Engine speed: 2,400 rpm
Power: 84.66 PTO hp
Transmission: Hydro (with two-speed
  sliding-gear auxiliary)
Weight: 13,840 pounds (6,278 kg)

Rear tire size: 18.4x34

Serial Numbers: Model 826

Beginning S/N	Year
7501	1969
8153	1970
16352	1971

Left: This 1969 Farmall 826 has an eight-speed manual transmission with Torque Amplifier. Owner: William Smith, Spencerville, Indiana

Above and right: *This 1970 Farmall 826 tractor has a diesel engine of 358 ci (5,867 cc) and the hydro-static transmission. Power brakes, power steering, and a Category II three-point hitch were standard on the 826. Owner: Tim Johnson, Atlanta, Indiana*

The Farmall 966, 1971–1975

International Harvester unveiled the 66 Series tractor lineup in the fall of 1971. The Farmall 826 (along with the Farmall 1026) was an aberration in the IH tractor numbering system. This was corrected in 1971 by replacing the 826 with the 966, which was essentially a nonturbocharged Model 1066.

With its naturally aspirated 414-ci (6,784-cc) diesel, the 966 was in the 90 to 100 horsepower range. This engine featured a wet-sleeve, which simplified an engine overhaul when the time came. In 1973, competition forced IH to increase rated engine speed to 2,600 rpm, giving the 966 close to 101 horsepower. Because IH was dropping the Farmall moniker at this point, almost all of these tractors were Internationals not Farmalls. The standard transmission for the 966 was the eight-speed sliding-gear mechanical type with optional Torque Amplifier, driven through a new 8-inch (20.3-cm) clutch. The fully hydrostatic transmission with the two-speed sliding-gear auxiliary was also available. With the Hydro, stepless speeds of from 0 to 8 mph in low range and 0 to 20 mph in high range were available with the engine speed set at 2,600 rpm.

Standard features of the Farmall 966 included deluxe fenders, a full instrument panel, a differential lock, and a heavier front axle. Options included dual rear wheels, front wheel assist, Custom, or Deluxe cab (the Custom version was discontinued in 1973), and a high-clearance version.

Models and Variations

Model	Years Built
966	1971–1975

Specifications: Model 966

Engine: Six-cylinder
Fuel: Diesel
Bore & stroke: 4.3x 4.75 inches
  (109.22 x 120.65 mm)
Displacement: 414 ci (6,784 cc)
Engine speed: 2,400 rpm
Power: 96.01 PTO hp
Transmission: Sixteen speeds forward
  (with T/A)
Weight: 13,500 pounds (6,124 kg)

Specifications: Model 966

Engine: Six-cylinder
Fuel: Diesel
Bore & stroke: 4.3x4.75 inches
  (109.22x120.65 mm)
Displacement: 414 ci (6,784 cc)
Engine speed: 2,400 rpm
Power: 91.38 PTO hp
Transmission: Hydro (with two-speed
  sliding-gear auxiliary)
Weight: 12,875 pounds (5,840 kg)

Specifications: Model 966

Engine: Six-cylinder
Fuel: Diesel
Bore & stroke: 4.3x4.75 inches
  (109.22x120.65 mm)
Displacement: 414 ci (6,784 cc)
Engine speed: 2,600 rpm
Power: 100.8 PTO hp
Transmission: Sixteen speeds forward
  (with T/A)
Weight: 13,670 pounds (6,201 kg)

Rear tire size: 16.9x38

Serial Numbers: Model 966

Beginning S/N	Year
7101	1971
11815	1972
17794	1973
22526	1974
28119	1975

The 1975 Farmall 966 was available only in the diesel version. It used a 414-ci (6,784-cc) six-cylinder engine of about 95 horsepower. This one has a Year-A-Round cab.

Chapter 6

Six-Cylinder Farmalls Over 100 Horsepower

The Farmall 1206, 1256, 1456, 1026, 1066,

1466, 1566, Hydro 100

The Farmall 1206 Turbo Diesel, 1966–1967

The 1206 used the same-displacement engine (361 ci/5,916 cc) as in the 806, but the 1206 was a completely different unit. The tractor was beefed up and strengthened to withstand the increased power that a new turbocharger provided. (IH's Solar Turbines Division produced the turbocharger.) A hardened seven main crank was used with larger oil passages. A larger radiator fan and air cleaner was used, and the transmission and drive train were also strengthened.

The 1206 came out three years after the 806 and was styled somewhat differently. A welded tubular grille replaced the cast grille of the 806. At first the paint on the 1206 looked much like the 806, but after the first year, IH added a gold-script "Turbo" decal on each side of the hood and a metal "Farmall 1206" emblem.

The standard transmission for the 1206 was an eight-speed sliding-gear mechanical type. The Torque Amplifier power shift and dual rear wheels were optional. A single 1,000 rpm PTO was included, as was either a Category III three-point hitch or a Fast-Hitch, flat-topped fenders with lights and handholds, and a deluxe seat. The 1206 was the last of the big Farmalls offered with a tricycle front.

Models and Variations

Model	Years Built
1206 Turbo	1966–1967

Specifications: Model 1206 Turbo

Engine: Six-cylinder
Fuel: Diesel
Bore & stroke: 4.125x4.5 inches
  (104.76x114.3 mm)
Displacement: 361 ci (5,916 cc)
Engine speed: 2,400 rpm
Power: 112.6 PTO hp
Transmission: Sixteen speeds forward
  (with T/A)
Weight: 13,580 pounds (6,160 kg)

Rear tire size: 18.4x38

Serial Numbers: Model 1206 Turbo

Beginning S/N	Year
8626	1966
12731	1967

The first over-100-horsepower row-crop tractor available to the farmer was the turbo-charged Farmall 1206 diesel. It produced almost 113 hp during its Nebraska test. This is a 1967 model. Owner: Ron Neese

The Farmall 1256 Turbo Diesel, 1967–1969

The 1256 Farmall was a mildly restyled version of the 1206. A Schwitzer turbo replaced the Solar unit, since IH had sold off the Solar subsidiary to Caterpillar. The 1256 got the new 407-ci (6,670-cc) diesel engine, as had the 856. Horsepower at the PTO now exceeded 115, and drawbar horsepower exceeded 100.

As with the 1206, the transmission on the 1256 was an eight-speed gearbox (actually, a four-speed unit with a two-speed sliding-gear auxiliary). With Harvester's Torque Amplifier, partial-range power shift, sixteen speeds forward were available. Tractor speed at 2,400 rpm ranged from less than 2 mph (3.2 kph) to more than 19 mph (30.6 kph).

New shifting controls on the 1256 (and others in the 56 Series) eliminated complaints about the straight-line shift pattern for the range lever. To get to reverse with the old system, the range lever had to pass through low range. When shifting from reverse to high, low-range gears clashed, a problem that was especially annoying when operating a front-end loader. The new pattern was a traditional "H." The driver selected high and low ranges by moving the lever up and down; reverse was selected by moving it to the right and down.

Wedgelock wheels, a tilting steering wheel, and a high back seat with hydraulic suspension were all standard on the Farmall 1256. Factory installed ROPS (Roll-Over Protection System) were first offered on the 56 Series Farmalls.

Models and Variations

Model	Years Built
1256 Turbo	1967–1969

Specifications: Model 1256 Turbo

Engine: Six-cylinder
Fuel: Diesel
Bore & stroke: 4.32x4.63 inches
  (109.73x117.6 mm)
Displacement: 406.9 ci (6,668 cc)
Engine speed: 2,400 rpm
Power: 116.12 PTO hp
Transmission: Sixteen speeds forward
  (with T/A)
Weight: 13,810 pounds (6,264 kg)

Rear tire size: 18.4x38

Serial Numbers: Model 1256 Turbo

Beginning S/N	Year
7501	1967
7703	1968
8444	1969

Above and facing page, top: *The 1968 Farmall 1256 had the same displacement (406.9 ci/6,668 cc) as the 1206, but with a Schwitzer turbocharger rather than the Solar unit. Horsepower was up to 116 in the Nebraska test.*

Left, both photos: *Factory cabs were becoming the norm by the late 1960s. This 1969 Farmall 1256 has the Year-A-Round cab and dual rear tires. The 407-ci (6,670-cc) turbo diesel produced 116 horsepower at the PTO.*

The Farmall 1456 Turbo Diesel, 1969–1971

The Farmall 1456 was the most powerful Farmall to date. An improved 407-ci (6,670-cc) turbo diesel with dry sleeves produced over 130 horsepower at 2,400 rpm.

Because of the boost in horsepower over the Farmall 1256, IH made a considerable amount of changes to the 1456, adding a larger radiator and cooling fan, and widening and strengthening the transmission and final-drive gears. The rear axles were now 3.5 inches (8.9 cm) in diameter to handle the torque. New brakes with 11-inch (27.9-cm) discs replaced the 8-inch (20.3-cm) discs of the 1256. A new two-door cab became available for the 1456, allowing entry from either side of the tractor.

Although production of the Farmall 1456 got off to a slow start, 5,582 were delivered before the end of production.

Models and Variations

Model	Years Built
1456 Turbo	1969–1971

Specifications: Model 1456 Turbo

Engine: Six-cylinder
Fuel: Diesel
Bore & stroke: 4.32x4.63 inches (109.73x117.6 mm)
Displacement: 406.9 ci (6,668 cc)
Engine speed: 2,400 rpm
Power: 131.80 PTO hp
Transmission: Sixteen speeds forward (with T/A)
Weight: 17,350 pounds (7,870 kg)

Rear tire size: 18.4x38

Serial Numbers: Model 1456 Turbo

Beginning S/N	Year
10001	1969
10405	1970
14149	1971

Above and facing page: *While the 1970 model 1456 looked much the same as the 1256 it replaced, it was all-new from front bumper to the drawbar. In its Nebraska test, the 1456 made 131.8 PTO horsepower. Owner: Marty Thieme*

Farmall 1026 Turbo Diesel, 1970–1971

The Farmall 1026 was only offered with hydrostatic drive, the first 100-plus horsepower tractor to be so offered. Except for a new grille, the 1026 was similar to the 1256.

Models and Variations

Model	Years Built
1026 Turbo	1970-1971

Serial Numbers: Model 1026 Turbo

Beginning S/N	Year
7501	1970
9707	1971

Specifications: Model 1026 Turbo

Engine: Six-cylinder
Fuel: Diesel
Bore & stroke: 4.32x4.63 inches
   (109.73x117.6 mm)
Displacement: 406.9 ci (6,668 cc)
Engine speed: 2,400 rpm
Power: 112.45 PTO hp
Transmission: Hydro
Weight: 14,975 pounds (6,793 kg)

Rear tire size: 18.4x38

Farmall 1066 Turbo Diesel, 1971–1976★

The Farmall 1066, which replaced the 1026, used the new 414-ci (6,784-cc) turbo diesel. It was available with either the mechanical or the hydrostatic transmission. Front wheel assist (FWA) was an option, as was the deluxe two-door cab.

   A stronger front axle allowed the 1066 to carry side-mounted tanks. Other standard equipment included an instrument panel with real gauges, improved lights, a dual-shaft PTO, and an electrically operated differential lock.

★Note: 66 Series Farmall serial numbers are intermixed with Internationals. After 1973, tractors badged "Farmall" become increasingly rare and disappeared completely during 1975.

The 1975 1066 weighed 7 tons (6,350 kg) in working trim. It was powered by a 414-ci (6,784-cc) wet-sleeve six-cylinder turbo diesel that produced over 115 horsepower.

Models and Variations

Model	Years Built
1066	1971–1975
1066 Hydro	1971–1975

Specifications: Model 1066

Engine: Six-cylinder
Fuel: Diesel
Bore & stroke: 4.30x4.75 inches
   (198.22x120.65 mm)
Displacement: 414 ci (6.784 cc)
Engine speed: 2,400 rpm
Power: 116.23 PTO hp
Transmission: Sixteen speeds forward
   (with T/A) and two-speed sliding-gear
   auxiliary
Weight: 15,170 pounds (6,881 kg)

Specifications: Model 1066 Hydro

Engine: Six-cylinder
Fuel: Diesel
Bore & stroke: 4.30x4.75 inches
   (198.22x120.65 mm)
Displacement: 414 ci (6.784 cc)
Engine speed: 2,400 rpm
Power: 113.58 PTO hp
Transmission: Hydro (with two-speed
   sliding-gear auxiliary)
Weight: 13,190 pounds (5,982 kg)

Rear tire size: 18.4x38

Serial Numbers: Model 1066

Beginning S/N	Year
7101	1971
12677	1972
24205	1973
34949	1974
46855	1975
56672	1976

The 1975 Farmall 1066 used the turbocharged version of the 414-ci (6,784-cc) six-cylinder wet-sleeve diesel. Owner: Wilson Gatewood

The Farmall 1466 Turbo Diesel, 1971–1976★

Models and Variations

Model	Years Built
1466 Turbo	1971–1973

Specifications: Model 1466 Turbo

Engine: Six-cylinder
Fuel: Diesel
Bore & stroke: 4.30x5.00 inches
 (109.22x127 mm)
Displacement: 436 ci (7,145 cc)
Engine speed: 2,400 rpm
Power: 133.4 PTO hp
Transmission: Sixteen speeds forward
 (with T/A)
Weight: 16,230 pounds (7,362 kg)

Specifications: Model 1466 Turbo
(tested as an International)

Engine: Six-cylinder
Fuel: Diesel
Bore & stroke: 4.30x5.00 inches
 (109.22x127 mm)
Displacement: 436 ci (7,145 cc)
Engine speed: 2,600 rpm
Power: 145.77 PTO hp
Transmission: Sixteen speeds forward
 (with T/A)
Weight: 16,660 pounds (7,557 kg)

Rear tire size: 18.4x38

Serial Numbers: Model 1466

Beginning S/N	Year
7101	1971
10408	1972
15533	1973
19746	1974
25404	1975
29516	1976

The Farmall 1466 replaced the 1456 in 1971. It featured a new turbocharged 436-ci (7,145-cc) diesel engine, which produced 145 horsepower. The eight-speed transmission (four plus two) had sixteen speeds available (including eight reverse speeds) when the optional Torque Amplifier partial-ratio power shift was included. In 1973, IH upped the rated speed of the 1466 to 2,600 rpm, raising the output to 145.77 horsepower.

The 1466 featured the beefed up front

end of the 66 Series tractors. Also available as an option was the improved cab, featuring better visibility and soundproofing. The electric differential lock was not available, and only the 1,000 rpm PTO shaft was provided.

*Note: 66 Series Farmall serial numbers are intermixed with Internationals. After 1973, tractors with a "Farmall" badge became increasingly rare and disappeared completely in 1975.

With a 436-ci (7,145-cc) six-cylinder turbocharged diesel engine of 145 horsepower, the 1972 Farmall 1466 featured a beefed-up front end. The Deluxe Cab, with improved visibility and soundproofing, was available.

Farmall Hydro 100 Turbo Diesel, 1973–1976*

As was the case of the Hydro 70 being a rebadge of the 666 Hydro, the Hydro 100 was rebadge of the 966 Hydro. This rebadging was done to avoid direct comparisons between the two transmission types. Hydrostatic transmissions are by nature less efficient than gear drives and therefore have less pulling power.

The flexibility offered by the hydro more than made up for the losses as some farmers saw it, but still there was resistnce to buying a tractor for more money that could pull less. The 1066 Hydro was also the same tractor as the 966 Hydro, but turbocharged.

It is not clear from records just how many of the 5,431 Hydro 100s were actually labeled "Farmall." While serial numbers are unique for Farmalls as opposed to Internationals of the same series, this does not seem to be the case with the Hydro 70 and 100. Most likely, those made in 1973 had Farmall badges and those made in later years had Farmall badges until such badges ran out of stock. A new white hood strip identified these models.

*Note: After 1973, tractors badged "Farmall" became increasingly rare and disappeared completely in 1975.

Models and Variations

Model	Years Built
Hydro 100	1973–1976

Specifications: Model Hydro 100

Engine: Six-cylinder
Fuel: Diesel
Bore & stroke: 4.3x5.00 inches (109.22x127 mm)
Displacement: 436 ci (7,145 cc)
Engine speed: 2,400 rpm
Power: 104.17 PTO hp
Transmission: Hydro (with two-speed sliding-gear auxiliary)
Weight: 12,765 pounds (5,790 kg)

Rear tire size: 18.4x38

Serial Numbers: Model Hydro 100

Beginning S/N	Year
7101	1973
7727	1974
10915	1975
12434	1976

The Farmall 1566 Turbo Diesel, 1974–1976★

The 1566 replaced the 1466. Harvester boosted the horsepower to 160 by increasing the injector stroke and turbocharger pressure. To handle the increased torque, the final-drive planetary reduction gear set was redesigned. Rated speed remained at 2,600 rpm. A new six-speed transmission with Harvester's Torque Amplifier gave twelve forward speeds. The 1466 sported a new IH-built cab. Options included air conditioning and an eight-track stereo. Farmall-badged 1566s are rare, but there were some.

★Note: 66 Series Farmall serial numbers are intermixed with Internationals. After 1973, tractors badged "Farmall" became increasingly rare and disappeared completely in 1975.

Models and Variations

Model	Years Built
1566 Turbo	1974–1976

Specifications: Model 1566 Turbo

Engine: Six-cylinder
Fuel: Diesel
Bore & stroke: 4.30x4.50 inches
    (109.22x114.3 mm)
Displacement: 436 ci (7,145 cc)
Engine speed: 2,600 rpm
Power: 161.01 PTO hp
Transmission: Twelve speeds forward
    (with T/A)
Weight: 18,260 pounds (8,283 kg)

Rear tire size: 20.8x38

Serial Numbers: Model 1566 Turbo

Beginning S/N	Year
7101	1974
7837	1975
12589	1976

Chapter 7
Eight-Cylinder Farmalls
The Farmall 1468 and 1568

The Farmall 1468 Diesel, 1971–1974

The Farmall 1468 was built between 1971 and 1974, with just fewer than 3,000 delivered. It was the first Farmall with an eight-cylinder engine.

The 1468 was essentially a Farmall 1466 with a DV-550 (nominally 550-ci/9,013-cc) diesel V-8 engine supplied by the IH truck division. The engine was naturally aspirated and produced a PTO horsepower of 145. The DV-550 was set up to run on only four cylinders at idle or low loads. Cylinders one, four, six, and seven received fuel under these conditions, and the other cylinders had their valve lifters vented so the valves remained closed.

The 1468 featured an eight-speed manual transmission and an optional Torque Amplifier.

Competitor Massey Ferguson had introduced the first V-8 conventional tractor since the Funk-Fords of 1951. Massey Ferguson introduced their Model 1150, powered by a Perkins 511-ci (8,374-cc) diesel, in 1967. An upgraded version, the Model 1155, came out in 1973. Oliver also announced its Caterpillar V-8–powered Model 2255 in that year. Hence, IH quickly modified the DV-550 to fit in the 1466 chassis.

The 1974 Farmall 1468's 550-ci (9,013-cc) V-8 diesel engine had a bore and stroke of 4.50 x 4.3125 inches (114.3x109.53 mm) and a rated speed of 2,600 rpm. Owner: Paul Baughman

Models and Variations

Model	Years Built
1468	1971–1974

Specifications: Model 1468
Engine: Eight-cylinder
Fuel: Diesel
Bore & stroke: 4.5x4.31 inches
   (114.3x109.47 mm)
Displacement: 548.7 ci (8,992 cc)
Engine speed: 2,600 rpm
Power: 145.9 PTO hp
Transmission: Sixteen speeds forward
Weight: 16,310 pounds (7,398 kg)

Rear tire size: 18.4x38 duals

Serial Numbers: Model 1468

Beginning S/N	Year
7201	1971
7239	1972
9109	1973
9670	1974

Some 2,900 1468s were built between 1971 and 1974. Under light or no load, the injectors fire only four of the eight cylinders. All eight fire as the load increases. This is a 1972 model.

The Farmall 1568 Diesel, 1974–1976

The 1568 replaced the 1468. The naturally aspirated DV-550 engine of the 1568 was upgraded to just over 150 hp by head and piston changes. This is a 1975 model.

Models and Variations

Model	Years Built
1568	1974–1975

Specifications: Model 1568

Engine: Eight-cylinder
Fuel: Diesel
Bore & stroke: 4.5x4.31 inches
  (114.3x109.47 mm)
Displacement: 548.7 ci (8,991 cc)
Engine speed: 2,600 rpm
Power: 150.7 PTO hp
Transmission: Twelve speeds forward
Weight: 17,350 pounds (7,870 kg)

Rear tire size: 20.8x38 duals

Serial Numbers: Model 1568

Beginning S/N	Year
7201	1974
7821	1975

The Model 1568 replaced the 1468 in 1974. At least a few carried Farmall badges, but for the most part, the Farmall brand name was dropped in 1973. The 1568 was the same tractor as the 1566, except a naturally aspirated V-8 engine replaced the turbocharged six used in the 1566.

The tractor was an improvement over the 1466 and 1468 models in that a stronger planetary final drive was included to cover the increased horsepower, and a six-speed transmission replaced the eight-speed unit of the earlier series. The Torque Amplifier was a common option, doubling the ratios available.

Index